DIM TRAILS

BY RAY HUNTER

2007

For Further Information or to order book:
Ray Hunter
605-347-0218
1220 Cedar Street, Apt# 409
Sturgis, SD 57785
or
Casey Hunter
605-892-4228
P.O. Box 2015
Belle Fourche, SD 57717

FIRST EDITION 2007

Sand Creek Printing, Sturgis, SD

**Cover features the DoubleX Cowboys in the 1950's (from left)
Burrell Phipps; Baxter Berry, owner; Charlie Larson, cook; Ray Hunter;
Lyle O'Brien; Art Thode**

STORY BEHIND THE COVER PICTURE

I was workin' for Baxter Berry on the XX Ranch in 1959. An outfit out of Denver, Colorado got a hold of Bax, and they wanted to take some pictures to make an old time western movie. They sent a photographer up to take the pictures. He came out to the ranch the night before, and in the morning when we were getting ready to go, Lyle got up on a buckskin horse that blowed up and bucked like a scalded dog. The man made a run for his pickup to get his camera. By the time he got it, it was too late.

He did get one good picture of all the cowboys by the wagon. On the left is Burrell Phipps on a horse called Squirrel. If you're guessing we called him "Squirrel" because he was a little squirrelly, you're right. I rode the horse to school four and a half miles when he was three, and he bucked all the way to school, and all the way back.

I quit and left, lookin' for new country. They put Squirrel in Gib Peck's string. He bucked quite a lot when Gib first started riding him, and he finally quit. Stan Anderson and Gib Peck were riding down the road ditch one day, were going to cross over and go through a gate when a car came down the road and around the corner. Squirrel got to looking at the car, got to shakin' a little bit, and just fell over. Gib had quite a sense of humor, and said to Stan, "You didn't know I was ridin' a trick horse, did you?" At the time of this picture, Squirrel was 14 years old, and broke good.

Baxter Berry, the fellow standing on the left, was the owner of the outfit. Next to Bax is Charlie Larson, an old time cowboy and roundup cook who was in his 70's at this time. I'm leaning on the mess box; next was Lyle O'Brian, and Art Thode is riding the other horse, a 14-year-old called Preacher. Art was a brother to the first champion bronc rider, Earl Thode.

The photographer wanted us to build a fire and go about our usual tasks around the wagon. Baxter started building a fire and looked up at me and said, "Why don't you drag up some wood?" I was riding a little sorrel horse that day that was wild and would kick at me whenever I reached for my stirrup. I knew he would run away, but I thought if I could get him to run by camp, I'd undally my rope and leave the wood by the fire. I hooked onto the wood, and there was a fork in the branches. I was getting' along alright until one of the forks stuck in the ground and turned the pile of wood over. That was more than he could stand, and he broke and run. In order to get to camp I had to hit the creek crossing. I missed the crossing, got the rope under the horse's tail, and he bucked me off right on the creek bank.

The photographer wanted us to bunch the cows up and stampede them over a little hill. He took his camera on a tripod and went down over the hill to get set up. When we put the cows down over the hill, they got to runnin', and he got scared and run off and left his camera. The cows knocked it down and rolled it to the bottom of the hill. We done everything we could—we put on quite a show for him, but I don't believe he got a picture of the action. The pictures he did get had a part of the pickup in it or something else that shouldn't have been in the picture. ●

ABOUT THE AUTHOR

This is a book of stories told in a unique homespun cowboy way. These stories are true, not fictional, and I can personally verify them as I was actually there in many of them.

These stories are for anyone who is or ever wanted to be a cowboy and for all who cherish the cowboy lifestyle.

Ray Hunter is a life long friend—extending back to grade school days in a small, one-room, country schoolhouse. Ray was in the seventh grade while I was in the fourth. He had to ride horseback about four miles to school. He would come to school with frost on his eyebrows and eyelashes, and his lunch would sometimes be frozen. He never missed a day! One of these stories tells you why!

Hunter, in his younger years, lived with many different families. His father had died when Ray was young and Ray's mother left him with various "foster parents."

Hunter, in his younger years, lived with many different families. His father had died when Ray was young and Ray's mother left him with various "foster parents." Ray finally found a home with Baxter and Lyndall Berry on the Double X Ranch and they became his secondary parents. Many of these stories reflect happenings on the Berry Ranch. The cowboy life took priority over higher book learning so Ray never finished high school. After leaving the Berry Ranch, he joined the Marines; and after his completion of duty, he returned to the ranch.

LYNDALL BERRY

He has had many different occupations: cowboy, ranch owner, bar owner, construction worker, ranch foreman, auctioneer, rural mail carrier, sale barn manager, real estate broker, family man, and he worked for and on many ranches. So you see, he has had experience in the things told in these stories. Throughout this book, Ray shares with us some of his personal experiences and encounters.

This book no where tells all the stories that he can tell. When I asked him why some of his stories are not included in this book, he replied that some stores are best left untold! Like the time he spurred the buckskin paint horse, his day as a caterpillar driver, and the time he left some of us sitting on steps of the White River school house after a dance. There are many more!

I have had many good times with my friend, Ray Hunter, and cherish many memories of the times we had working together. Memories may fade a bit, but many memories never die.

Hunter's stories and laughter were always entertaining at any gathering. They were the life of the party. Ray is a people person who loves life and if he was around, you might not see him but you could hear his laughter.

When reading this book of stories, I hope you enjoy reading them as much as Ray enjoyed telling them.

By Stanton Anderson

RAY HUNTER IN 1948
RIDING HAPPY

DEDICATION AND INTRODUCTION

I would like to dedicate this book to Baxter Berry, who was like a father to me; and also, to Tom Berry, Paul Berry, Burrell Phipps, Gib Peck, and to all the old timers and cowboys in the bunk houses along the way that had a hand in raising me; to Paul Brunch and Stan Anderson for a lifetime of friendship. A lot of these stories were told to me by old timers of the old days in South Dakota; and some of the stories are of my life and times. You will find stories of some of the horses that I knew. I was a cowboy and rancher all my life. I never knew or wanted anything else. I'm not a writer, but want to put these stories down before they are gone with the wind. Saddle up, take a deep seat, put both feet in the stirrups, and ride along with me.

BAXTER BERRY

A special thanks to Lorna Moore for the artwork in the book; and to Patty Byers—this book would never have been written without her.

Ray Hunter

HELPING WILBUR

I rode the rough string for a couple of big ranches, broke a few horses, entered a few rodeos and even drove on black ice. But the most dangerous thing I ever did was helping Wilbur.

Late in the fall a few years ago Wilbur called me up to go up in the Black Hills and help get some cows that had got off his permit. I couldn't figure out a good excuse and I was used to taking chances so I agreed to go. Takes his pickup and trailer and has a four wheeler in the front of his trailer and one horse in the back. I took my pickup and trailer and one horse. We go out by Pactola Dam. I parked my pickup and loaded my horse into his trailer. Now if you have been to Pactola Dam and look off the East side you will see how steep it is. There is a little trail on the south side of Pactola Dam that goes down that steep mountain side. So we start down with the pickup and trailer and get on ice that was on the trail. It was like riding on a pair of skates. We skated down the mountain side going faster and faster. We hit a big bump, bounced and luckily came down a little up higher on the side of the mountain. The reason we were lucky was that there were two trees ahead of us. I hollered at Wilbur, "You better take a tree". The tree was about 10 inches through. We just straddled it, broke the tree off and jerked the roots up out of the ground. It all slowed us down

some but not a whole lot. The tree that broke off lit out in front of us. We run up on it and it slowed us down and finally stopped us. About another one hundred yards we would have run off a two hundred foot cliff.

I unloaded the horses which took quite a lot of the weight off the pickup. Wilbur got the pickup in low range and finally got to the bottom of the mountain. I'd had all of it that I wanted so I just walked and led the horses.

We spotted the cows we were after. Wilbur said, "I'll just jump on this four wheeler and go around and see if there are any more". All he did was spook the cows and get them wild. He came back, he got horseback and we went after them. Now the cows had split up. One bunch found a hole in the fence that some hunter had cut. Wilbur went after them. One bunch got up in the corner of the fence just below the dam. Now they really wanted to run, but I was lucky enough to hold them in the corner. I held them for about an hour and drove them up on the highway by Pactola Dam. I kind of had an idea where Wilbur would end up with his cows, at Snyder Ranch. I headed that way with mine. Sure enough Wilbur had penned his up there and I penned mine there too. We found another trail to get our pickup and trailer up out of there. Then went and loaded the cows and headed for home. ●

THE YEAR NINETEEN NINETEEN

In the 1918 and the spring of 1919, chain banks came into the country and loaned about everybody money to buy livestock. In an area south of Belvidere, South Dakota, that ran maybe twenty thousand head of cattle, by late spring was stocked with over forty thousand. A man by the name of Ives came in and settled on Big Badland Table (later named Ives Table) with three hundred head of cows. Another man by the name of Paul Meyer came in and settled about a mile and a half from him with twenty five hundred head of Mexican steers on a little creek that was later named Paul Meyer Creek.

He brought in a young kid with him by the name of Claude Dale to ride on the steers. A lot of other ranchers in the area also moved in with their cattle. By the first of November, there wasn't a spear of grass or a weed to be found anywhere, and then it started snowing and turned into one of the worst winters in history. One of the ranchers in the area was Tom Berry, who had about 500 cows; he moved them east of there, where they'd put up quite a lot of hay. He hired two men to go over and take care of the cattle, each with a team and a saddle horse.

The area where the cows were was fenced, so it helped keep the strays and drifting cattle out. These boys hauled hay with a team and a pitchfork, feeding the cows every day, plus riding and keeping other drifting cattle on the move. Their names were Ted Thomas and Sam

Stoddard. After they'd been in camp a while, they both got mad and wouldn't speak to each other; one would get up early in the morning, cook his breakfast, do his dishes, and put the fire out, then go out to the barn, clean the manure out from behind his team, and throw the manure behind the other fellow's horses. The next morning, the other one would get up first and do the same thing. How they managed to stay in camp all winter without killing each other is a mystery!

Tom Berry was able to save most of his cattle. By spring, most of the cattle in the area had died or drifted out. Mr. Ives was too broke to leave the country, so he stayed most of the summer picking bones. You could get a dollar for a wagon load of bones in Belvidere. When he got enough money, he left the country. ●

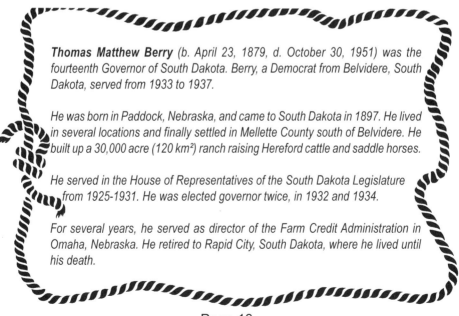

Thomas Matthew Berry (b. April 23, 1879, d. October 30, 1951) was the fourteenth Governor of South Dakota. Berry, a Democrat from Belvidere, South Dakota, served from 1933 to 1937.

He was born in Paddock, Nebraska, and came to South Dakota in 1897. He lived in several locations and finally settled in Mellette County south of Belvidere. He built up a 30,000 acre (120 km²) ranch raising Hereford cattle and saddle horses.

He served in the House of Representatives of the South Dakota Legislature from 1925-1931. He was elected governor twice, in 1932 and 1934.

For several years, he served as director of the Farm Credit Administration in Omaha, Nebraska. He retired to Rapid City, South Dakota, where he lived until his death.

WINTER OF 1936

The winter of 1936 went down in history as one of the coldest and longest that we ever had. I was eight years old and working for my room and board around Norris, South Dakota. We got up pretty early in the morning, cold and frosty, milked a bunch of cows and done the chores, then I walked two and a half miles to school, a little country school with about seven kids and a big stove in the corner. I walked home after school and done our chores. We lived in an old two-story frame house which had no insulation or storm windows. The kitchen had a big wood range stove that had a reservoir in it for water. It was always warm and damp in the kitchen, and the frost got about two inches thick on the inside of the windows, so we couldn't see through them. Every time we opened the kitchen door outside, a big cloud of damp warm air would go out.

The big old house was full of bedbugs, so all the bedsteads were set in cans with kerosene in them, and we fought bedbugs all the time, but it didn't seem we could keep them out of our beds, as they'd crawl up on the ceiling and drop down on our bed.

The big old house was full of bedbugs, so all the bedsteads were set in cans with kerosene in them, and we fought bedbugs all the time, but it didn't seem we could keep them out of our beds, as they'd crawl up on the ceiling and drop down on our bed. These folks had an old kerosene lamp that they'd set on the table, and they read the Bible every night in German for an hour before we went to bed.

These folks were Germans who had come from Russia; they knew nothing but hard work, and could live where other people couldn't make it. It was a long old winter, and I was sure glad to see spring.

GOING TO SCHOOL

I went to stay at Baxter and Lynall Berry's the fall I was thirteen years old. I started school at the Phipp's school, four and a half miles away, and rode there. Being the only kid at the ranch with a bunch of cowboys, they kidded me to no end, and were always getting me into some kind of jackpot or another.

They got to teasing me about going to school and finally said if it was five degrees below zero or colder, I wouldn't have to go. I liked that just fine because I didn't like school, and it was a lot more fun staying home and helping them.

Art Thode stayed in the bunkhouse with me and part of the time Chad Addison. The first thing I done in the morning after school started, was check the thermometer. It was always above five below. I would trot and lope right along to school wherever the snow wasn't too deep. And when I got there, a lot of mornings, the icicles on my horse's nose would be three inches long, and the hair on both sides of his body would be frosty white.

About twenty years later, I stopped out to visit old Art Thode. He had a camp job riding for Baxter Berry. We got to talking about old times. Finally he said, "You know you should have amounted to something, 'cause I sure done my part. You never missed a day of school when I was at the ranch with you. I knew the first thing you'd do every morning, was check the thermometer, so I just got up first and held a match under it!"

A SHEEPSKIN COAT

The 1930's were a hard time for everyone. There wasn't much money around so people got by the best they could with what they had. My dad died in 1934 at the height of the depression. In 1936, my mother made arrangements with some people on a farm in Mellette County, South Dakota, to keep me. I worked for my room and board milking cows and doing other chores.

The winter of 1936 was long and cold. I got so cold I didn't think I would ever be warm again. We lived in an old two-story frame house. In those days there was no insulation and I don't know of any storm windows. The frost would build up on the inside of the windows to two and three inches. There was no way to see out through them. If somebody drove up in the yard, generally in a team and wagon, you couldn't see out to see who it was.

Long about Christmas time a big brown box came from Sears Roebuck, something my mother had ordered for me for Christmas. I looked and shook it and wondered what it could be, and finally on Christmas morning I got to open the box. Inside was the most beautiful sheepskin coat I had ever seen. I took it out of the box and ran my hand down over the moleskin outershell and over the sheepskin collar. Oh, how wonderful it felt.

Inside the box was a sheet of paper that said the coat cost $8. The thought of an $8 coat was beyond anything I could comprehend.

This was in a time when a big hayrack load of hay cost 50 cents, a gallon of kerosene cost two cents, and you could buy a pound of liver for a penny.

I walked two and a half miles to school and with doing the farm chores, how wonderful that sheepskin coat felt. I would pull the collar up around my face and snuggle down into the warmth and the luxury of that wonderful coat.

Oh, what a sad day, two years later, when I outgrew my wonderful sheepskin coat. I finally agreed to give my sheepskin coat to one of the neighbor boys. I can still remember the glow and look of satisfaction on his face as he put on my sheepskin coat.

A Happy Christmas!

WINTER OF 1949

In 1949, I'd been out of the service a while, and had got a job working on the Berry Ranch. I was staying at a cow camp in the middle of a pasture about the size of a township. When I got up the morning of January second, we were in a big blizzard, and it stormed for three days. Down in this camp there was quite a lot of shelter, since there were pine and cedar trees all around. I had two saddle horses tied in the barn, and it was a treacherous and dangerous job just to get down there to take care of them. The snow would whip around my eyes and mouth until I could hardly see or breathe. When the storm let up, I started riding, because there were about 2000 Hereford steers in this pasture.

My horses were good, hard, and grain-fed. I put on a lot of clothes, tied my pantlegs down over my overshoes, as my horse would get bogged down in the snowdrifts and if I jumped off, my boots would get plum full of snow.

The storm had drifted them into shelter, and the snow was so deep around them that they wouldn't come out on their own. Some of the drifts were 20 feet deep and 100 feet long so we had to break a trail in order to get them out of there. My horses were good, hard, and grain-fed. I put on a lot of clothes, tied my pantlegs down over my overshoes, as my horse would get bogged down in the snowdrifts and if I jumped off, my boots would get plum full of snow. They got so's as soon as they got bogged down, they'd stop and I would jump off. Generally I'd try to tie my throw rope on the end of my bridle reins so I could get far enough in the lead, because I'd be wading in snow clear up over my waist and the horse would go to lunging and plowing snow. If I got too close, he'd knock me down in the snow and get on top of me, tromping me into the snow. I broke lots of trails and got steers up on the ridges where the wind had blowed out some grass. On some of these ridges there was a lot of yucca, which in this country, we call soapweeds. They'd stick their head down into the middle of a soapweed and wrestle it around until they broke it off, then they'd drop it, turn it around so the spines were sticking away from them, and eat it. Their heads were all green from the juice out of the soapweeds. One big soapweed would fill up a steer.

In the township, it was kind of hard to find all the steers, as some of them had gotten pretty well ganted up, and would stand right there and starve to death if I didn't break a trail. We never opened any water for them, and the grazing and soapweed was all the feed they got, and we had very little loss. I'd go over and help Bax every so often, as he was riding on a bunch of cows, calves, and yearling steers. Once in a while we'd find a pretty thin cow and weren't able to drive her very far, as she'd wear out quick. We always tried to carry a little cake with us when we rode, drive one of those old cows about so far, and feed her some of that good cake; we'd eventually get her home on feed. When we left home in the morning, we never got back until evening, getting nothing to eat all day. I don't believe that I was off the ranch until the middle of April.

WINTER OF 1951-52

I was working for the Jones Ranch over by Midland, South Dakota, on Brave Bull Creek. The Joneses had leased down on the Red Stone on the Pine Ridge Indian Reservation, about 15 miles south of Belvidere, South Dakota. We went down about a week before Thanksgiving to work that country. We had to gather about 300 yearling steers and trail back to the ranch on Brave Bull. While we were there, it got cold and stormy. We started back the day before Thanksgiving in a storm. We trailed into the north all day against wind and snow, about a thirty mile drive. We got to a pasture on the Jones Ranch called West Fork, and trailed our extra saddle horses on home, which was another seven miles. It was  after dark when we got to the ranch, with about a foot of snow on the ground. Generally after we got all the cattle on winter pasture, we had time to put up wood and get ready for winter, but winter was here. The camp I was on would winter about 300 calves and light yearlings, and we started hauling hay to them it seemed like right away. I had a little wagon at my camp, and I'd hook a team to the wagon and break a trail down to the feed ground. Then I would go down to the creek, which didn't run much water, so I'd have to chop a lot of ice to find the

---

The first of January we got a blizzard that was the "grand daddy" of them all. It caught me on the feed ground, and I just barely made it home.

---

water; then I'd go hook onto my hayrack and pitch on three loads of hay and string it to the calves. It took all day and it'd generally be after dark when I got home.

The first of January we got a blizzard that was the "grand daddy" of them all. It caught me on the feed ground, and I just barely made it home. There were some people in the area who didn't, and were found froze after the storm. It stormed for about three days, and the

snow got about three feet deep, so when I went down to feed with my little wagon, I'd have to break a trail from the hay to the feed ground, then I'd hook onto the empty rack, and follow that trail out to the feed ground. If I caught the end of my feed rack on a snowdrift, my team wouldn't pull it, as they were pretty balky and didn't want to pull anyway.

I always carried an ax and a scoop shovel with me on the way out in the morning. If I'd spot tree limbs sticking out of the snow, then on the way home I'd stop to cut some off so I could load them, and I'd throw them down by the house. We had a 32-volt wind charger electrical system, and by the porch light I could see to cut wood. I'd go take care of my team, then go to the house, eat supper, and cut wood. I always tried to keep 4-5 days wood supply cut ahead. I was newly married, and we had a little baby; his diapers froze every night hanging over the stove, as you could throw a cat out through the house anywhere, and I never heard one complaint out of my wife. We went to town about the first of April, and we had a party.

THE SPRING STORM

In 1979 I bought a little ranch north of Edgemont, South Dakota, and operated that ranch until 1984 when I sold it and leased a place out west of Belle Fourche, South Dakota. That place had about 10,000 acres. The only building on the place was down on the Belle Fourche River, so I set my camp up there, as I had a little camper.

I shipped my cows up the middle of April; they were just getting located when it started to rain, on the 28th day of April. It rained all day the 28th, all day the 29th, and then on the 30th it turned to mixed rain and

snow. On the 31st, the wind shifted to the northwest and it started to blizzard. It blizzarded for two days. When it was over, the snow was about two feet deep, and the mud about a foot deep. We couldn't hardly get around with anything but horse-back. I gathered my cows the day before it started to blizzard, and throwed them down in some shelter on a south slope. I had been trying to cake these cows, but they were chasing green grass and partially shed off. I got on my horse as soon as the storm was over, trying to move cows out of the snow and up onto ridges. I had already lost quite a few cattle. When I got them up on the ridges, some of them were so cold that they just stood and shook, and would finally just fall over, slide down the hillside, and die. I think out of 250 head of cows, I lost 60 cows and about that many calves. I had never seen anything suffer so much in my life as I did then. It took quite a while to get over, emotionally and financially. That same storm killed hundreds of cattle and thousands of sheep, so maybe I was one of the lucky ones. •

BERRY FAMILY RANCH

After working for the Berry family off and on for 30 years—and many of these stories took place on their ranch—I would like to give you a little history of them and the ranch. Baxter Berry's grandfather was a frontiersman of Scottish ancestry, an early-day settler in northern Nebraska, I think in about the 1870's. I believe Tom was born in about 1875. He told me one time he was about 10 years old when he seen his first cowboy who came up from Texas with a trail herd of cattle for the Indians on the Rosebud Reservation in South Dakota with the Niobrara River being the Reservation boundary.

Tom Berry moved to Gregory County, South Dakota and homesteaded about 1906. Tom told me the grass was stirrup high and thicker than the hair on a dog's back, as they hadn't started plowing yet. Tom then moved to Tripp County, South Dakota and from there, to Mellette County when they opened it up for homesteading in 1913. Tom and his sister each got a quarter section of land. Tom made the move

because the country was rougher, and he didn't think there would be quite so many farmers. The family came with team and wagon, and Baxter, who was eight years old, helped trail the cattle and horses. From this start, the ranch grew to over 100,000 acres at the main ranch, with another ranch in North Dakota, and another north of Wall, South Dakota.

Tom Berry was elected governor of South Dakota in 1932, and turned the operation of the ranch over to Baxter. Baxter and Lindell were married in 1933, and due to their hard work and commitment, the ranch prospered. Baxter spent quite a lot of time searching for breeds of range cattle that could stand the cold and hard conditions of South Dakota. One of the breeds was the Scotch Highland cattle; I believe the first

bunch was bought in 1943, and many purchases made through the 40's and early 50's. Some cattle were imported from Scotland and Canada at that time. I believe the herd of Highland cattle finally reached upward to 200. The Berry's sold a lot of Highland cattle in the 50's and 60's, and these went to about every state in the Union.

As to the operation of the Berry Ranch, the ranch ran about a 1000 head of cows, which calved in April. We never weaned any calves, but they were all separated from the cows in March. The ranch also

300 head of cows in North Dakota; these calves were separated from the cows and brought to South Dakota in the fall. The same was done on the ranch north of Wall, which ran about 150 cows. We generally purchased about 400 calves to go along with those we raised. The steer calves were sold the fall they were two years old. We generally kept 150 bulls and 100 head of saddle horses. Most of the time we never fed the yearling steers anything. The cows were given forty percent cottonseed cake in the winter time. The only thing that was ever hayed was some of the smaller calves that we brought in from other ranches or which we bought. The rest of the calves were wintered on cake and grass. On the main ranch we ran about 3500 head of cattle, this number depending on the year.

Baxter Berry ran a strictly cowboy outfit.

WRITTEN FOR BAXTER BERRY

while he was hospitalized at Sturgis, SD
—by Stanley Sloan, formerly of Interior, SD

April 1975

Old Pal, how times have changed
And everything been rearranged.
We never thought it was so tough
Though often heard that times were rough.

We kept a bronc up on a stake
And got five bucks for those we'd break.
They weren't gentle ponies then
But full grown, wild, and hard to pen

Wrangling horses was a chore
But one of those things that we bore.
Remember the frosty mornings, and the sky cold gray
It wasn't fun, but it sure saved hay.

There was water in the nearby creek
We broke the ice with a heavy stick.
We dragged our wood up with a horse
And swung the axe as a matter of course.

Our ambition then was a good outfit
Saddle, chaps, and boots that fit.
And a private horse of some renown
That we'd ride when we went to town.

So long ago it sometime seems
As though it was the stuff of dreams.
But half a century can't get rid
The memory of the things we did.

Later, of course, our ambitions grew
Though cow work and broncs was all we knew.
Wages was the start we had
Too bad we didn't have a wealthy Dad/.

I didn't start this with the intent
To make it sound like a lament.
Now I feed my gentle horse some grain
And stay in out of the rain.

I cuss if the automatic heater don't work right
Or the hot water goes off in the night.
I don't ride now so very far
When I go to town I drive a car.

I like to tell of the rugged past
But to try it now, I wouldn't last.
It's one of the things I hate to admit
But Damn it all, I just ain't fit.

Baxter Berry was born March 7, 1906
He died August 10, 1975
Buried at Belvidere Cemetery in Jackson
County, South Dakota.

THE HENRY HORSES

Old Man Henry was a one-eyed Texan who brought a line of horses up from Texas, most all good quarter horses, but Mr. Henry failed to keep the papers up on most of them. He bought a ranch between Philip and Cottonwood, South Dakota, along Highway 14. Most of these horses were duns, and after a few years, about every cowboy in that area was riding one. I looked at the Henry horses a couple of times, but was never able to buy one. The last time I looked, Mr. Henry had quite a few horses, and had a big tall albino colored boy breakin' a bunch to ride. I watched him a little while, and decided that he was quite a horsebreaker and had such a way with horses that nobody else would be able to ride them.

A friend of mine, Jerry Ferley, had a little dun horse which he called Clyde. I traded for Clyde, mostly hoping that one of the girls could run barrels on him, but that wasn't to be; Clyde wasn't a barrel horse. We went to roping on him instead; we roped on him quite a lot, but he was awful hot in the box, and we had to be pretty careful with him, or he'd fall over backwards on us in the box. After lots and lots of work and time, we finally got him over it. We roped on him for several years. Casey and I were team roping in SDRA, and finally won the state championship in 1976. I turned old Clyde out in later years and pensioned him; he was around for several years, fat as a butterball.

Old Clyde

Page 28

RIVER HORSE

In my string of horses, the most important was the river horse. When I worked for the Antler Ranch in southeast Montana, we swam the Bighorn River lots of times. It seemed like the best place to swim the river was at a little place called St. Xavier. I think there was a post office and a little store there, although all the times I crossed the river, I was never in there. The Antler Ranch had mostly all Mexican cattle in 1945, and most of these cattle had been trailed from 500-1000 miles to the US-Mexico border.

They were broke to drive, and would go whatever direction we pointed them. There wasn't much to crossing a river with them, as they all swam good. A bigger problem was finding a horse that was good in the water. The Bighorn River was always swimmin', sometimes a lot higher and wider than other times. I went through my string of horses, trying to find a good river horse. Before we rode into the river on any of them, we got off and loosened the cinch, because they needed

room to blow up. We had to watch the bridle reins, as the current would catch them and start jerkin' on the bit in the horse's mouth, and would turn the horse over backwards. I finally found a big, stout, sorrel horse that was really good in the water. When I got him in the river, I would pull the bridle off, and with a rein around his neck, I could guide him. If the current was real bad, once in a while I would turn the lead steers back, and they would go to swimming in a mill. I could swim him out there, break up the mill, then turn him around and swim him back. I always tried to save him so he'd be fresh for the river. Seems it was so long ago, I can't remember what we called him, but I sure can remember the horse. ☙

DOLLY

Dolly was a loud-colored, good lookin', sorrel and white paint mare. She ran down in the Badlands of South Dakota in a stud bunch, and never had a colt. She was big, fat, and beautiful, nine years old, and had never even been halter broke. We penned these horses one day, and Baxter Berry said to me, "If you want to break her to ride, I'll just give her to you." She was just as wild as a deer, but broke out real easy and got gentle to handle. I rode her for about a year, and the next summer I went to the Frontier Days Rodeo in White River, South Dakota. This was 1949, and White River had a pretty big rodeo at that time, so I decided to take her there, and bulldog off her. I took a friend of mine along and talked him into getting into the bulldoggin' too. Neither one of us had ever jumped at a steer, but didn't think it

looked too hard to do. I was entered in the saddle bronc riding too, so when they called for the "doggers", I was up before my friend, and talked an old-time cowboy, Vern Whittaker, into hazing for me. Vern always had a good doggin' team, but I wanted to ride Dolly. We got backed into the box, and when I nodded for the steer, Vern and the steer got right out, but I couldn't get old Dolly to go. She finally broke and ran, and I caught them about the middle of the arena; and as I went by, I got off, hit the ground, rolled over, looking up, and all I could see was feet, so I just kept on rolling out of the way. After watchin', Don wouldn't ride Dolly, but got on Vern's doggin' horse, and made his run. It looked like he got down real good, except he hoolihanded the steer, and had his arm tangled up in the bridle rein, jerking the horse down on top of him and the steer both. We had to pack him out of the arena. We had taken the roundup bed with us, so took that up to a sale barn they had, and threw it on the floor. Don spent the rest of the rodeo right there on that bed, but I think he done a lot better than I did, as he had a pretty girl from over on Pass Creek take care of him. I rode Dolly again the next day, but she wouldn't run to the steer; I rode one bronc and bucked off another, didn't win any money, but it sure seemed like we had lots of fun. Old Dolly got so she wouldn't let anyone come near her or touch her after the rodeo; it was just too much noise and too many people, so I never took her to another one.

JONES BRANDING

The Jones Ranch had their headquarters on Brave Bull Creek by Midland, South Dakota. In the 1940's they had a big lease on the Pine Ridge Indian Reservation, where they ran about 1200 cows. Most all the cows were Herefords at that time. They went down around the first of June with a roundup outfit to brand up these calves. The ranch owner, Tom Jones, was an old time cowman, born in the state of Washington, I believe around 1875. He trailed horses out of Washington and Oregon east to meet the homesteaders as they came west. He'd trail horses as far east as Minnesota, where they corralled horses at night and built fires to try to keep mosquitoes off them—the mosquitoes about drove them crazy. He was quite an old character, and after he got a car, he never went nowhere without it. He had an old black Chevrolet car, and drove it just as hard as it would go.

When we went to the Reservation to brand, the weather turned bad, it got to raining, and they ran out of grub. Tom had the cowboys hook a team to his car, and they pulled it up out of the Badlands onto some gravel hills. Tom got Art Thode with him, and they were going to go to Belvidere, South Dakota to resupply. They stayed on the sod and gravel hills until they got to Black Pipe Creek. Tom stopped the car up on the ridge overlooking the creek; they got out and laid a tarp on the ground, ran the car up on the tarp, pulled it up over the hood and over the top, then tied it in place. The creek was running a lot of water, and there was no bridge. Tom wound the old car up and came down off that ridge, hitting the creek as hard as they could go, never slowing down. He drove out on the other side, and it was about a

quarter mile to a gravel road. They stopped the car, took the tarp off, and went on to Belvidere to get groceries. On the way back, they stopped on the gravel road, pulled the tarp back up over the car, raced through the creek, but didn't make it quite to the top of the ridge before they got stuck in the mud. There was an old man living on top of the hill by the name of Fred Brownsworth; he had an old team that had pulled many a car to the top of that ridge. He charged a dollar for every car he pulled out. Art and Tom drove back the same way they'd come, staying on the sod and the gravel. They loaded the groceries up in the wagon and went down to camp. When the weather straightened up, we got the calves branded. There was an old saying in this country, "When Tom Jones made up his mind, he was a hard man to stop!"

SCOUT

I first laid eyes on Scout, a little brown and white paint yearlin', when Baxter Berry bought him at the St. Onge South Dakota sale for $35 ; he was kind of feathered legged and big footed, showing he had some draft horse background. We started Scout when he was three years old, but the boys said he was so gentle and kind that we turned him out until he was four years old. Casey went to ridin' him, and he told me that every time a cow looked at Scout, Scout got all excited,

so I thought I'd take and ride him to see if he'd make a cuttin' horse. The fall he was four years old I went to workin' herd on him, as we bunched all our cattle outside and worked them horseback. Workin' cattle outside on a four-year-old was hardly ever heard of, as most four-year-olds weren't broke good enough. He just had a lot of natural cow. When he got to be about six years old, they had some cutting contests around the country, and I got to haulin' him to some of them. I worked him at the Civic Center in Rapid City, South Dakota, several times. When I'd ride him into the arena, the crowd would really clap for him, as he was the only horse entered of his kind; the rest were all well-bred quarter horses. I won and placed in several cuttin's on him around the country. I had five different kids ride him in high school rodeo, and every one made it to the finals.

When Scout got to be about 14, I decided to sell him; I took him to the Stock Show sale in Rapid City and a doctor's wife by the name of Deb Dixon bought him. After she bought him she came out and wanted to ride him. She crawled on him bareback and rode him around, then slid off and threw her arms around his neck and started bawlin'. I asked if she liked the horse. She said, "I just love him! And I've been looking for a horse like this for so long." They never did work any cattle on him, just rode him or hooked him to a buggy and drove him a little. She had two or three little kids. I saw her not long after she'd bought him, and she said the kids would be out playing near old Scout, and he'd lay his head on their shoulder and follow them around. She kept Scout until he was about 30 years old, then had to put him down. I saw her a couple of years later, and she said, "If you ever got another Scout, let me know, as I'd like to have him." I said, "Deb, there'll never be another Scout."

HORSE MANURE IN THE MILK BUCKET

When I was 15 years old, I went to work for Baxter Berry for my room and board. Baxter ran a big ranch on the Rosebud and Pine Ridge Indian Reservations in South Dakota, and it was a cowboy outfit. I was a horse wrangler and jingled (wrangled) the horses every morning before breakfast on a green two-year-old colt. I could generally get one of those colts away without bucking if I was careful.

There was an old cowboy working there by the name of Art Thode, and he milked the cow at the same time. I would always try to get away when Art wasn't around. I'd get a colt saddled up, and look all around, trying to spot old Art. I'd get the colt up in the corner and step on, and here would be old Art—didn't seem like I could ever keep track of him. Art would holler at me, say "Kid, what in the ..... are you doing around here? Get after the horses!" and would throw the milk bucket under the colt. The colt would blow up and buck out the gate; he never did get me bucked off, but when the colt would finally quit buckin', I'd be hanging on to the saddle horn with both hands, lost both stirrups, both bridle reins, and my hat. So what do you do, sitting on a colt all swelled up, and you're about to fall off? I'd generally slide off, and was lucky enough to grab hold of the bridle rein, and get back on. That was just generally at the start of the ride. When I got after the horses, generally as I raised my arm to spook the horses, it would scare the colt and he'd run away, but eventually I'd get them gathered into the corral.

I can remember Baxter's wife, Lyndall, asking Baxter how Art got horse manure in the milk bucket; I'm sure Bax knew, but never told Lyndall! One morning Art threw the milk bucket under a colt, the colt kicked it over to the side of the corral and smashed it. Lindell asked Baxter how a cow could kick a bucket up like that. This went on all spring until I got so I could set up and ride, and he never bothered me again.

THE CBC

The CBC was a big horse outfit, and around 1920, was closing out. They had about 400 head of Percheron studs out by Eagle Butte, South Dakota. The outfit up at Eagle Butte was ramrodded by Ernest Edson. He'd run a lot of big outfits around the country, I believe the Diamond A and the Turkey Track were some of them.

The CBC also had some sheep at this time. A young boy by the name of Clinton Harry was herding a bunch of buck sheep around this camp, and would put the bucks in the corral every night. He said Ernest Edson and a bunch of cowboys brought those Percheron studs and put them in a little pasture around that camp for castrating and branding. There were two or three big corrals there at camp; they'd put a little bunch of studs in a corral every morning, then they'd take a number nine wire around the bottom of an open gate about a foot off the ground. Ernest Edson would cut out one of those studs and bring him just as hard as he could run over that number nine wire. The wire would trip him, and down he'd go, and some cowboys would jump on him, get a hold of him, and tie him down. They had a vet there who would do the cutting. They'd turn the horse loose, re-stretch the wire, and do another one. I believe that cuttin' studs this way would separate the men from the boys! There were a few of them that didn't get tripped, and they had to be roped. Clinton said he was sure glad he was a sheep herder after watching them!

THE WILD BUNCH

In the spring of 1950 the Jones Ranch over by Midland, South Dakota had a little bunch of wild mares, most of them two-year-olds that they wanted to trail over to the Pine Ridge Indian Reservation. They had lost most of their Indian leases by this time, but still had a pretty good chunk of deeded land. At this time, Ralph, the son of oldtimer Tom Jones, was managing the ranch.

These mares were wild and hard to handle. We decided to gag them, which is a way to cut off their wind. We got them into the corral, four-footed them and tied them down. We got a good ash stick, about two inches through and eight inches long, which we ran in their mouth, took a good soft rope which we tied onto one end of the stick, took the rope up over the top of their head, and tied it to the other end of the stick. We pulled the stick way up in their mouth and tied it. We did that to the wildest mares. We tied an old wagon burr in their foretops, which we found out didn't do much good. The next morning at daylight we started out with those little mares. It's about 30 miles to the Reservation. There was Richard Doud, Wayne Hare, and myself. The gags worked real good; the mares handled well, and we made good time. We got to the pasture where we were headed in early afternoon, and penned the mares in a corral there. There was a part Indian fellow by the name of Oliver Rooks there who worked part time for Jones, riding their cows through the summer. We rode over to Oliver's and talked his wife, Edith, into fixing us dinner. After dinner we went back over, four-footed the mares, and took the gags off them. There were about 12 of these mares, and I think we put gags on four of them.

The gate in the corral went right out into the pasture where we wanted the horses, so we opened the gate and turned the mares out, but they turned and ran back through the fence into Oliver's pasture. As we were watching, they turned and ran out the other side, back where they were supposed to be. We thought it was kind of funny, though Oliver didn't. We stepped up onto our horses and headed for home, getting back to the ranch about 8:30 that night. ◖

Catching horses in a rope corral.

THE TWO-BELLIED SORREL

In southeastern Montana is a country they call The Little Mountain Country. It lies north of the Big Horn River between the Big Horn Mountains and the Prior Mountains. There are little steep mountains and some with flat tops with rimrocks along the sides.

I was seventeen year old and just started working for the Antlers. The only reason I could get a job cowboying there was that the good hands were all off fighting the Second World War.

We left the main headquarters ranch with a bunch of yearling steers, probably about five hundred, to trail to the Little Mountain Country. The main ranch headquarters were on the Little Big Horn River north of Wyola, Montana. We trailed the steers across to St. Xavier Montana, where we swam the Big Horn River.

Frank Greenough was the wagon boss and was catching horses for me to go in my string. The first morning out he caught me a big bald-faced sorrel horse. The horse had an extra big belly full of Montana grass – which is where he got his name "Two-Bellied Sorrel". It took Bill Greenough and another cowboy ahorseback to drag him out of the ropes. Frank put a hackamore on him and slid it right up under his eyes. It wasn't good daylight yet and I'd always heard horses don't buck as hard before daylight. When I finally got him saddled, I got on him and he bucked me right off.

The horse had an extra big belly full of Montana grass – which is where he got his name "Two-Bellied Sorrel".

I caught Two-Belly and waited until they turned the cavvy out of the rope corral. When he was looking at the horses trotting out of the corral, I stepped on him. He was big and goosey and ran away. When I finally got the run out of him, he was still real goosey and kept kicking the spurs on the heels of my feet. Now, as you can guess, I didn't trail many cattle that day as I just loped him around the herd getting so I could ride him. When noon came I was sure glad to get off.

We trailed the cattle on a few more days and finally got up to the Little Mountain Country where we turned them loose. Frank was still catching horses for me, and he caught the Two-Bellied Sorrel again for me that morning. When we finally got him out of the ropes and got him saddled, I got on and he was traveling just like he was walking on eggs, grabbing himself, looking back at me and kicking my feet.

We'd turned the yearlings loose and was going to go over the mountains and ride some other country to check for more cattle. We got along pretty good until we got on top of the mountains where he was still just as goosey and grabbing himself. We got on top of a flattop mountain and he broke and ran. He ran around the top of the mountain about four times and then headed right straight across it. When we got close to the edge, I just gave him his head. He dropped his head down right on the edge of the rimrock. About 1000 feet off down into the canyon was WhoDo Creek. After a good look, he finally turned and ran down back on to the flat and quit running.

All the other hands had just pulled up and were watching the event. There was one old cowboy in the bunch they called Old Ed. He said, "Son, You'll never be no whiter when you die." Another cowboy spoke up and said, "And you'll never be no closer and not do it!" ●

GATHERIN' THE WILD BUNCH

About 1950 we trailed a little bunch of mares over to the Reservation for the Jones Ranch, and turned them loose in a pretty big pasture with a lot of rough country in it. These mares ran over in that pasture for about 10-12 years. When we trailed them over, none of them were supposed to be pregnant, but they were, so they went on to have colts. Nobody bothered those horses in all that time; I guess they forgot about them.

They finally decided one spring that they were going to have to go over and do something with them, so Stanley Sloan, Baxter Berry, and Ralph Jones were some of the crew to go. These horses were about as wild as horses can get; the cowboys ran some, and finally got a few of them into the corral. The rest of them they ran and roped, trying to relay them (one cowboy would run them a ways, then another cowboy would wait and take his place to run them a ways, and finally  the third or fourth cowboy could get a rope on one). Then, just because you got a rope on one, didn't mean it was easy to get her to the corral! The little colts were so wild when they separated from their mothers, they would run into the brush and try to hide like a little fawn. These horses were just like antelope: they wouldn't stay in a bunch. The crew was about out of saddle horses because they'd run their horses down pretty good. A neighbor by the name of Shorty Ireland came over to help; he had a Jockey Club horse that was a topnotch filly chaser. When he got after one of those wild horses, he'd just cut it out, and away they'd go, running off banks, jumping creeks.........Shorty took some wild rides, but that old horse never quit. I don't know how many horses he ran down so the cowboys could rope them! I think he ran down at least 10 or them. He was one great horse, and we maybe wouldn't have gotten them all if it hadn't been for him. ●

COWBOY SPORT

Back around the First World War, the Badlands of South Dakota was still pretty wild country. On the Rosebud and Pine Ridge Indian Reservations there were a lot of part-Indian and white cowboys that were good hands and awfully wild. They ran lots of horses in the Badlands in those days. Most were the little wild mustang type. They would generally run horses for several weeks. When they got enough of them gathered up and broke to handle they would trail them to Nebraska where there was a market for them. They would generally take a couple of weeks on the trail up and back. Most of these little mares were bred to big studs as the bigger horses were worth more.

Baxter Berry and his dad, Tom, rode up to the Brown Ranch one day. Baxter was about 8 years old at this time. The Browns had a big round corral packed full of wild mares. They were just as wild as horses could get. Setting around on the top rail of the corral was a bunch of cowboys – mostly of the Brown and Rook families. The mares were packed pretty tight in the corral. A cowboy would jump down on the back of a wild mare, grab her by the mane, she would try to buck and run. But they were packed tight enough they couldn't really get to goin', but were still be hard to ride. When she got next to the corral again, he would climb back up on the rail and another cowboy would get on another wild mare. They did this all afternoon, laughing and hollering.

MATADOR COWS

Tuffy Eaton who ran the Valentine, Nebraska auction, traded for a bunch of cows off the Matador Ranch in Texas, and shipped them to the Arnold Ranch at Cody, Nebraska. In the late summer of 1964 Tuffy traded about 250 cows to Baxter Berry. These cows were all Herefords. In early October he sent some of us to trail them home. In that crew was Shorty Jones, Ski Rasmussen, Stan Anderson, and myself. Neil Peck was the cook, Gib Peck was the wagon boss. We loaded up the wagon with supplies and beds. It was a light load so we

just took one team and a small cavvy of horses. The ranch we started out from was 15 miles South of Belvedere, South Dakota. The going was good till we got South of the Little White River. Then we got into the sand. The wagon wheels went into the loose sand up to the hub. We took three saddle horses and hooked our ropes to the tongue of the wagon to help the team pull. About half way between the river and the ranch was a high ridge of sand hills. It was all uphill. When we got to the top of the ridge we started running on to dead cattle.

We counted about 20 head from there to the ranch. The cowboys that were trailing the cows, got behind them and let them run, according to Billy Pourier. We had to stop the horses and let them blow quite often. We traveled that way until we got to the Arnold Ranch, which was about 20 miles. Our horses were played out and so were we.

Billy Pourier was the cow boss on the Arnold Ranch. He told us where we could camp and turn our horses loose. We started to set up our tent, Billy told us we could move into a house there if we wanted to. We declined the offer and went ahead and set up our tent. That night the wind came up and blew the tent down and blew sand into everything. We were glad to move into the house the next morning.

The wind blew the sand all the next day. We had never been in a sand storm before. The sand hit your face with such force it would take the hide off.

The crew at the Arnold Ranch was to brand the cows for us. But due to the storm we had to lay over a couple of days. The first day of the layover was on a Saturday. We heard that Billy's daughter, Boots, was going to Cody to see her boyfriend. We talked her into giving us a ride to town. Everybody went but Gib.

It was quite a night. I bet the town of Cody still remembers it. Boots picked us up about 1:00 am. The sand hill roads are rough and full of sand. A couple of the cowboys riding in the back got sick. Boots finally got so she wouldn't stop. The cowboy in the middle of the back seat grabbed the other two cowboys by the belt and hung them out the windows so they could be sick. The two in front were singing. Boots stopped about every two miles to tell us to shut up or she would make us walk. The whole ride home was that way. I'll bet Boots won't haul any cowboys again. We always said we did more for the two that got sick than any preacher ever could.

Billy told us there was a little pasture about eight miles from the ranch. We could put the cows there by the afternoon. It was a good start for home the next morning. He also told us that these cows were awful wild. The people that gathered them and brought them to the ranch couldn't hold them and they ran all the way. The result was all the dead cattle along the trail. They had run themselves to death.

Gib got us boys together and told us we were going to have to handle the point on them and turn them back into a mill. We were young and had never handled any cattle this wild before. Gib was a top hand

and we sure listened to him. We started the cows, milled them, and started them again. They sure wanted to run on us. By turning the point back we kept them under control. The whole eight miles went this way. The next morning we handled the cattle the same way. They run and milled about all day.

We still had the wagon to move and our team was played out. We got a tractor and pulled it to the top of the big sand ridge. It was downhill all the way to hard ground. Then we got along alright. We trailed for two and a half days and finally got them broke to drive. We had them broke to drive so well we trailed them right to the little town of Norris.

About a year later I read a story in the Western Horseman about the Matador ranch in Texas. They said whenever you seen a Matador cow she was running. That sure was the truth. •

SHOCKING GRAIN

Right after the drought in 1937 the crops were pretty good and we had a lot of grain to cut. Now in those days there was no such thing as a combine. All the crops were cut with a binder. Bonick's, the people I worked for, had two binders. One they pulled with the tractor. The other they pulled with six horses. A binder would mow it and tie it up in a bundle and kick it back out on the ground. These bundles all had to be picked up and put in shocks. Shocking grain was hard job. You walked and picked up the bundles till you had enough to make a shock. Then all these bundles had to be pitched on a bundle rack and hauled to the thrash machine which separated the grain from the straw. The straw was blown into big stack. The grain was loaded in wagons and hauled to the granaries. It was all done by hand.

I was nine years old and helping to shock. The bundles were heavy and it seemed like there was a rattlesnake under every one. Alex rode up to talk to Mr. Bonick one day. Alex Whipple had a big lease off to the south and east of us back in the rougher country. He had it stocked with steers. Alex had a reputation far and wide as a good cowboy and was quite a roper. I really got to looking his outfit over and I remember it well to this day. He was riding a crop-eared brown horse. His saddle was slick and shiny from use. The thing I really noticed was that he had a silver mounted ladyleg bit and spurs to match. After looking Alex over pretty good I decided that someday that was going to be me.

FRANK GREENOUGH, ANTLER COWBOSS

Antler Ranch was in Southeast Montana. The headquarters was north of Wyola on the Little Bighorn River. The ranch was owned and operated by Matt Shurge. He had a big part of the Crow Indian Reservation leased: the lease started at the Little Bighorn River and ran to the Pryor Mountains, running about 10,000 Mexican steers. I worked there in 1945 as a kid of 17. The cow boss on the Antler Ranch was Frank Greenough, who had two brothers, Turk and Bill, who were famous bronc riders. I never saw Frank ride a bronc, but he sure was a good wagon boss, knew how to gather the country and run a crew.

The Antlers pulled their roundup wagon out right after the fourth of July and stayed out until about Thanksgiving. They tried to ship out a trainload of fat steers about every two weeks. Frank generally had a crew of 10-40 men at different times. A lot of cowboys working for other outfits came to the wagon with a little string of horses, with their bed tied on one; they were called "reps." They came to gather different brands when we were in their area. When they got their cattle gathered they would take their little bunch of cattle and their horses and trail for home. At times we'd have 200-250 horses in the cavvy, a lot of cowboys riding three to four horses a day.

Frank would start a circle to gather cattle early in the morning and have cattle on the roundup ground by nine o'clock. Everybody would go in and change horses, some of the young cowboys riding broncs would go on another circle and the rest would go to the roundup ground to start working the herd. Cowboys would bring the cattle for the next circle to the roundup ground and the circle crew would head for camp to eat and change horses. They would go on what they called a short circle. The rest of the cowboys would go on working the rest of the herd, move camp and trail the holding herd to the new roundup ground. Most overnight camps had little traps built with four-wire fences to hold the holding herd and cavvy at night, so we wouldn't have to stand guard.

Frank managed all this with the help of a few old hands who knew the country. They could guide the new hands around, and help keep them in the right place when they were on circle. Frank had some really good cutting horses. I remember one real well, a black horse with a big white bald face that he called Headlight. One of the things I remember well about Frank is he would run a loose horse half a day just to see you get bucked off again. While I was there, Frank left to go run an outfit of his own down north of Gillette, Wyoming, and his brother, Bill took over as cow boss. I think Frank got into some hard winters and finally went broke, which seems to be the destiny of a good cowboy. ◖

THE BUGLE

(Joe himself told this story to Baxter Berry and me in the winter of 1941 when we went to town to get our one winter haircut.)

The George Brown family were early day ranchers in Washabaugh County, South Dakota. Being part Indian, they could ranch on the reservation. So they got an allotment in the northeastern corner of the Pine Ridge Indian Reservation and settled on a big badland table. High badland walls surrounded it on three sides with the north end of the table going out onto a big flat. On the north end of the flat were high sand hills.

The only fence needed to fence it all in was a fence across the north end of the table; the rest being all natural barrier. The table still carries the family name of Brown.

In the summer of 1907 the railroad came to Belvidere, South Dakota. When the first train was going to come in George Brown, his older boys and some of the men decided they would ride to town and see the train. It was going to be in Belvidere about 4 p.m., so they were going to ride the 12-15 miles into town to see it as this was a very big event and nobody in the area wanted to miss it.

Joe, the youngest boy in the family, was about nine years old at this time and wanted to go along with the men pretty bad. But everyone decided he was too young to make the ride, so he had to stay home with his mother and sisters. Joe sat around awhile pouting and mad because he couldn't go. Finally when nobody was looking he snuck out and caught his pony.

He knew that town was north of the ranch, so he started out that way. He didn't go far into the sand hills and the White River breaks before he was lost. As he wandered around it got dark and he was getting plenty scared.

An Indian family by the name of Standing Bear had lived in the area just south of the Big White River. They had started a cemetery on a ridge and were just beginning to bury their dead as the white man did.

Joe rode up to the graveyard fence and sat on his pony awhile. Pretty quick he figured out he was sitting by a cemetery and got to seeing ghosts and spooks, so he ran his pony over the next ridge and sat on that ridge awhile.

About this time the wolves and coyotes started to howl; and Joe was really getting spooked so he rode his pony down across the draw to a ridge and then down across the draw to another ridge. Back and forth he went from one ridge to another.

While all this was going on George and cowboys had returned from town. Joe's mother was fit to be tied, so the cowboys changed horses and got ready to go look for Joe.

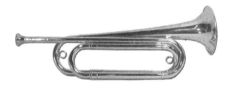

Now the Browns had an old bugle they got from an old Sioux warrior sometime before the turn of the century. Mrs. Brown gave the bugle to George so he could blow the bugle and call Joe that way. They rode down into the river breaks blowing the bugle every so often.

Joe heard the bugle all right and thought all hell had broke loose. The ghosts were really after him.

The cowboys would blow the bugle on one ridge and Joe would run his horse down across the draw onto the next one. This went on about all night. Finally they split into two groups, one group going down one ridge and the other going down another ridge, with George blowing the bugle. Joe ran his pony down across the draw and up into the other group of cowboys and they caught him.

You can bet that Joe wasn't caught out after dark for quite awhile. ●

THE ANTLERS COOK

In 1945, when the Antlers pulled their wagon out about the 15th of July, Harry Sharp was the cook. He was a little old bachelor who had a little place near Lodge Grass, Montana. I don't think he went home until the wagon pulled in just before Thanksgiving. When we first pulled out, the horse wrangler hadn't gotten there yet, so they had another kid and me wrangling horses. Harry was driving four up on the mess wagon, and they ran away every day for two-three days. The other kid and I tried to help him, but mainly just got in his way. As he got to hollerin' and cussin' us, he finally said, "I want you boys to stay plum away; I don't want you turning the lead team back over the wagon." The wagon was loaded pretty heavy, and Harry would put the brake on, so generally they would be run down in not too long a time. In two-three days, they quit running altogether. After we'd be out for a week or 10 days, the horses kinda settled down, even the broncy ones got better to handle. They stood in the rope corral a lot, waiting for the cowboys to come in and change horses.

They got trailed a lot between camps. About the only time they got to graze was at night, and the nights were pretty short.

The horse wrangler was boss of the cavvy. If the wrangler had a horse that was hard to handle or trail, he would tell the cow boss, and the boss would put a cowboy on him; he would ride him hard enough that he'd settle down.

The cook's day started about 2:30 in the morning, and ended about nine at night. Harry cooked for eight to 40 men, as in part of the country a lot of reps came to look for their cattle. Sometimes in the evening you would see two or three cowboys trailing a little string of horses with their beds tied on two or three. When we had a lot of reps, we generally had over 200 head of horses in the cavvy. It took two horse wranglers to handle them and help the cook.

The Antlers moved their wagon at least once a day, and sometimes twice. It didn't take Harry and one wrangler very long to set up a tent and get coffee on the fire. Wranglers got wood and water and helped the cook as much as they could. Part of the wrangler's job was to set up a rope corral and get the picket ropes set out for the night horses.

The right side of the wagon was the cook's area; and the right corner of the tent where his mess table and stove were was his area. You didn't get into it unless you were asked. I got along with Harry real good. If I had time, I'd help with the dishes and do whatever else I could to help him. Harry called me "the gallopin' kid", as I rode a bunch of broncs and I liked to keep them moving. Frank sent me on circle mostly, as I wasn't a very good hand around the herd. In the morning we rolled our bed and threw it down by the wagon. Cowboys always loaded the wagon. The last thing to be loaded was the stove, which sat right behind the mess box. Cowboys harnessed the horses and hooked them up. Harry got up on his seat and they handed him the lines. Harry wasn't a very big man, but was as tough as rawhide. There weren't many men who could do the work, cook for that many men, move camp once or twice a day, and drive runaway horses. Most cowboys at that time got $70-$90 a month. Harry was paid $25 a day, and earned every bit of it. ◖

KING OF THE COWBOYS

I seen a lot of cowboys and bronc riders in my time. This story is about a man that was a stock-hand, cowboy, and outstanding as a bronc rider. I first met him when I was about 14 years old. He was about 40 years old at the time and seemed to be in the prime of life – just as rough and tough as a piece of cowhide. His name was Stanley Sloan.

Stanley Sloan was born in 1900 in the Belle Fourche and Camp Crook area. His dad managed a ranch called the H.T. Ranch. They ran lots of horses and raised some remount horses. When Stanley was about five or six his dad would put him on an old thoroughbred stud. He would gather the old wild mares on that thoroughbred stud. Stanley started riding broncs at an early age. He learned to ride with hobbled stirrups. By the time he was 12 and 13 he was already an exceptional

bronc rider. He enlisted in the cavalry when he was about 15 years old. They had a lot of bad horses that nobody could ride. He told his sergeant that he could ride those horses if he had a stock saddle. So they sent and got his stock saddle. He rode those horses and a lot more before they discharged him for being too young.

I went up to old Frank Arbuckle's place north of Alzada. Now Frank was an old-time cowboy and after sizing him up, I thought he might have known Sloan. So I asked him. He said, "You bet I knew him! The first time I seen Sloan he was about 16 years old. The roundup wagon was parked just down the river from where I live now. Sloan and his brother came to the wagon with Sloan riding a bronc and his brother driving him on his bronc with the loose horses."

Stanley was a true cowboy. He cowboyed from New Mexico to Montana. While working in Montana on the Spear O Ranch (◄—O) they run out of broke saddle horses. The cow boss went over to a horse outfit and bought a bunch of big five and six year old part Percheron geldings. These geldings were all broncs. They penned them with the other horses, roped them, and drug them out of the rope corral. They tied them down and rolled them into a saddle. When they let them up Stanley and some of the other cowboys would be on them. That's how they broke them to ride.

About 1930 Stanley went to work for a Wild West show in Wisconsin. He worked every event plus trick riding. While working there he made a deal with the owner to come to South Dakota and run a bunch of horses. They shipped a bunch of mares by railroad to a little town called Weta. Stanley and his wife drove an old car up there to get the mares. The only saddle Stanley had was a trick riding saddle. He saddled up one of them old mares and trailed the rest to the ranch which was ten miles west. He raised remount horses for the Cavalry. He probably broke and rode from a 100 to 150 horses a year. They had to be rode and showed to be sold to the Cavalry.

Stanley came and helped on the XX Ranch every spring and every fall. He'd sold the ranch quite a lot of geldings that the Cavalry wouldn't take and they staked him to a lot of those geldings when he came to help. I seen Stanley rope a bull off a big black and white gelding he called Ribbons. When the bull hit the end of the rope Ribbons blew up and went to bucking. Stanley reached up and stuck him in the left shoulder and turned him into a spin. Every jump he'd take the slack of the rope up over his head and change hands on his bridle reins. When Ribbons got done bucking they were just like they were when they started. Most everybody I ever knew would have been tangled up so bad it would've taken them half a day to get untangled.

Stanley sold his ranch in the Badlands about 1942 and moved to Montana. He shipped his cattle. He and Chad Addison trailed his horses. Stanley sold that ranch about 1970 and retired, moving to Tacoma, Washington, where he passed away the spring of 1978.

Stanley was probably one of the best bronc riders and horsemen of his day. He was one of the last of the old-time hard-twisted cowboys. ●

SEVENTY-FIVE CENTS IN CHANGE

In the early 1960's we lived in a little town called Cottonwood, South Dakota. We were breaking a lot of horses at the time. My oldest son Casey was about 15 or 16 and he was helping me. The experiment farm, there by Cottonwood, bought a buckskin three year old colt. They wanted us to break him to ride for them.

The colt wasn't very broncy acting, but when we saddled him up, all he'd do was buck. If he untracked, he'd blow up and buck every time. We just saddled him up and let him pack an empty saddle around for four or five days.

He finally got so he could travel without bucking. We decided it was time to ride him. There was a rodeo arena right there close in town. We took him down there. There were some small pens back behind the bucking chute, and we put him in one of those to ride him.

Casey was pretty small and slim then and he was gonna ride him. Casey stepped up on him, and talk about a bronc ride! This horse bucked, spun, sucked-back, and kicked right straight over his head. He had Casey bowed down over the fork of his saddle with his head right in the colt's mane.

When he finally quit bucking, Casey rode him around the corral a bit and got off. We were standing there looking at the colt and talking when I looked down on the ground and seen some change. It was 75 cents - two quarters and five nickels. I showed Casey the money and he said, "I think that is my money." So I asked him where he'd had it, thinking it was in his shirt pocket. Casey said, "No, it was in my pants pocket."

I guess that's the first time I ever heard of change being bucked out of a cowboy's pants pocket.

One thing about Casey, he always knew where his money was, and kept good track of it; he quit riding broncs and became a banker, and a good one!

COPPER

I was breaking a bunch of colts for Baxter Berry one spring. In that bunch was a copper colored Roman nosed three year old Buckskin gelding. He was snorty and wild. You had to have a good hold on him and be careful around him at all times. He would strike you or kick you if given the chance. When you got off him he would try to jump by you or kick you. When you reached for the stirrups or cinches he would kick at your hand. The first time I rode him outside Baxter was always telling me about taking his rope down his first ride. So I thought if he could do it, I could too. The horse was so goosey that I hated to take it down and throw it. So I just undone it from my rope strap and let it drop. Things picked up in a hurry. He jumped and kicked straight over his head and went to bucking and running. Now there wasn't any way I was going to let go of that rope. Finally after going through this for a while I finally coiled my rope up and got it back on my saddle.

I finally got Copper broke to ride. But he never did get very gentle and never did quit snorting. He snorted at any and everything. A snorty horse is not much fun to ride. Bax finally took Copper over to the ranch to ride. He had a couple of girls over at the ranch and I think he wanted to show off.

Copper was finally traded off and I lost track of him. Four or five years later I went to help Gib Valandry brand his calves. Now Gib had a brother by the name of Paul. Paul was no cowboy. He had done some farming around Martin. I asked Gib how that old farmer could get along with that horse. He said he was deaf and couldn't hear him snort.

THE CLOTHESLINE 2

Back in the early 1960's, I was working for the Double X Ranch. We lived at a place called the Pines Cow Camp, down in the Badlands of South Dakota. We had a lot of pine trees, along with some cedars and cottonwoods. The house and the barn were down in the trees. It was a really pretty place. I built a clothesline when we first moved there, and didn't use the best of posts. My wife, Jean, was young and beautiful, and we were busy having babies. There was a good log bunkhouse about 50 yards from the house. There had been a rattlesnake around there, and I'd tried to get him several times, and I sure wanted to, because I had three young kids playing around there. I came by there one evening and was lucky enough to catch him and kill him. I got a shovel, and was filling in the hole, hoping it wouldn't happen again.

My oldest boy, Casey, was four years old, and wanted a horse to ride pretty bad. I didn't have anything gentle enough, but there was an old paint horse over at the ranch that was really gentle and liked people. Whenever we penned the horses, he would come over and try to walk on us to get our attention, so we'd pet him. We called him Lightning. The ranch owner, Baxter Berry, said "You'd better take him over to your place for that kid to ride." Old Lightning didn't like it down in that timber very well, but he and Casey seemed to get along all right.

While I was shoveling the hole full, I noticed Casey was leading old Lightning and talking to his mother. She had a big line full of diapers, since we had two young daughters, taking them down off the line and putting them in a basket. I went on with my work, and looked up just in time to see Casey lead old Lightning under the clothesline. The line caught on the saddle horn, and when it came tight, old Lightning jerked away from Casey and hit Casey with a front leg, rolling him out of the way. Jean was just reaching up to take a diaper off the line when old Lightning started his runaway, jerking the diaper out of Jean's hand, coming by the corner of the bunkhouse on a dead run, with clothes and clothesline hooked to the saddle horn. Diapers and clothes were whipping in the wind. He finally caught one of the clothesline posts on a pine tree, breaking the latigo, stripping off the saddle. When I saw that no one was hurt, I just fell down and went to laughing, and got to laughing so hard I couldn't quit. My wife didn't think it was very funny, and would hardly let me back in the house for two to three days.

PRETTY BOY

Pretty Boy was an Appaloosa, and I guess by the name, you can tell what he looked like. He was kind of red roan with a head that looked like it came off a dinosaur, and no mane or tail, but he was gentle and nice to be around, and you could do about anything you wanted to on him. I liked to ride Pretty Boy as a winter horse, because his hide was real thin like tissue paper; in winter time he grew more hair, which kept him from cinch-soring. We caked cattle mostly by horseback at that time, so about every other day I rode Pretty Boy somewhere or other to cake.

Stan Anderson had a horse out running in Cottonwood Basin in South Dakota, a favorite old pensioned saddle horse of his. He asked me if I'd kind of watch, and if it looked like "Old Popcorn" was getting too thin, to pick him up and bring him in, because Stan wanted to send him to a sale as being more humane than lettin' him get down beatin' his head on the ground and all the coyotes howlin' around him. So one day I saw Old Popcorn runnin' with a little bunch of horses, and I decided I'd better get him. We weren't trailin' those horses long, about four miles to a corral, so I thought I'd just sneak rope Old Popcorn. I got off and cinched up Pretty Boy, and when things came right, I roped Popcorn, but caught him clear down around the withers and the chest, and he wasn't named Popcorn for nothin'! When that rope hit him, he popped right out of there, and just about jerked Pretty Boy down. Pretty Boy's head and tail came together, and I was sure we were going down, but he got himself straightened up, and went to really paying attention. Popcorn settled down, and I led him on into the ranch.

When they sold the ranch, I bought all the horses, and I sold Pretty Boy to some feedlot operators in Iowa. For years after that, every time I would see one of them, they'd say, "Pretty Boy's getting old, and I don't know what we're going to do, because we can't run that feedlot without him." Pretty Boy was the kind of horse, wasn't a cowhorse, but was in the palm of your hand all the time. ●

JERKED DOWN

The Double X Ranch was working cattle out in the Badlands in the late summer of 1942. Some of the cowboys on that gather was Paul Berry, Burrell Phipps, Gib Valandry, Art Thode, Louis Beckwith, and was run by Baxter Berry. They bunched the cattle at the Paul Meyer Dam. There was a little trap by the Paul Meyer Dam. There was also a fence that run for several miles east and west. They put their extra horses in the little trap and after gathering the cattle all morning they needed a change. So they ran the loose horses up in the corner of the fence and just held their throw ropes in front of then as the horses had been broke to stand in a rope corral. Art threw a rope on a big sorrel bronc. The bronc wouldn't lead out of the horses. Louis Beckwith was saddled up on a four year old buckskin gelding he called Grandma. Louis said, "Give me the rope and I'll lead him out of there." Now Louis tied the rope to his horn and started to lead the bronc. Grandma was kind of peculiar and silly

about a lot of things. Louis finally got the bronc led out of the horses. Grandma goosed and ran away and the bronc right with him. They were headed right down the drift fence. The bronc finally jumped the fence. They went right down the fence breaking posts. Louis dropped the slack in the rope right down between Grandma's front legs. Grandma decided it was time to turn off, running just as hard as he could go. When he hit the end of the rope it jerked the bronc down and turned Grandma right straight over in a hoolahand, threw Louis out there about 20 feet. Baxter Berry run his horse out there and cut the rope. Louis didn't get hurt much but the sorrel bronc led pretty good after that and Grandma really got silly about a rope after that.

ONE OF SOUTH DAKOTA'S EARLY DAY PIONEERS

Joseph Rooks was born in Missouri in 1846. He fought in the Civil War with the North in the Seventh Missouri Cavalry. Joe enlisted in 1861 and was discharged in 1864. He came west with a group of pioneers and settled on Box Elder Creek in Colorado some 20 miles south of Cheyenne, Wyoming.

Joe freighted from 1866 into the 1870's from Denver, Colorado, to Deadwood, South Dakota. About 1866 Joe married a Larvie girl, the daughter of a French trapper and a Sioux woman. He traded a horse for her as was the custom of the time. Her name was Tingaliska, and she was a very beautiful woman. They had three children, but Tingaliska died in childbirth with the last child. She was an older sister to the woman Chief Crazy Horse had at the time he was killed at Fort Robinson.

In about 1873 Joe married again, to a part Sioux woman whose name was Kate Robinson. They raised the three kids from his first marriage, and also had 15 or 16 kids of  their own. Joe moved to Allen, South Dakota, on the Pine Ridge Indian Reservation in the early 1870's and served as the first Boss Farmer for the Indian Department. The job of the Boss Farmer was to take the bow and arrow out of the Indians' hands and replace it with plow handles. The community of Allen was on of the first population center in Bennett County.

Some time in the 1890's the Rooks family moved to Washabaugh County. Joe established a ranch on a big spring about 15 miles south of where Kadoka is now. This was all Badland country, a wild and rough place. Just east of the ranch was a large basin with Badland walls all the way around it, called Red Stone Basin. There were no white men allowed on the Reservation at this time, but they were allowed to settle on land allotted to Kate, his wife. About this time the Indian Department started issuing cattle to the Indians. The Rooks family got 18 cows, one bull, and a team of mares. Joe ranched on the open range. He never fed any hay, opened any water, or fed any other kind of feed. In these early days there wasn't a lot of stock on the range. There was a lot of grass and water everywhere. Most of the cattle were started from the southern Longhorn breed.

About 1900 a pool roundup wagon was used to brand calves in the spring and also to ship in the fall. Joe sold only dry cows and four-year-old steers. He also raised a lot of horses. Most of the horses carried the brand on the left hip. The horses were widely known for being wild, broncy, and bad to buck.

Joe Rooks sold out in 1918 and moved to Kadoka. Even with occasional hard winters and grey wolf problems, Joe sold over 650 head of cattle and 350 head of horses. It all started from the little herd issued to the Rooks family in the 1890's. He put his money in the bank in Kadoka, but the bank went broke in 1920. Joe died in the later 1920's, leaving behind a legacy of being a builder and developer of the West, and some 90 grandchildren.

WOLVES

Here are some stories told to me about wolves in the Badlands of South Dakota, which was one of the last strongholds of wolves. About the turn of the century when the boundaries of the Sioux Indian reservations were changed, the Big White River was the boundary on the North of the Rosebud-Pine Ridge Sioux Indian Reservations; the boundary ran on east to the Missouri River, south to about the Nebraska border, and on west to just east of the Black Hills. The reservation lands were restricted to white settlement until the year 1913. Cattlemen started trailing herds of cattle into South Dakota, including Thodes and Sears, who put a trail herd together and trailed in from Wyoming.

Somewhere between Wall and Kadoka along the Big White River, Hans Thode sent a cowboy by the name of Phil Black ahead to find a place to camp. Phil crossed a little creek and rode up on a big river

bottom on the north side of White River. The bottom was a big prairie dog town, and there were 18 big gray wolves on it. They came over, trotting along behind his horse, smelling his tracks, not the lease bit afraid of him. Phil was an old Texas cowboy who came up with the trail herds and had seen a lot of things, but never nothing like this. Phil was plenty scared of them and was sure glad when they went off and left him along.

Some people by the name of Berry came in and homesteaded on the reservation in 1913. Baxter Berry tells about the time when he was about eight years old, and they heard cattle bawling; they rode up on a Badland table and saw wolves running cattle about a mile away. His dad had a six shooter, so they ran their horses as fast as they could to try to chase the wolves away from the cattle. By the time they got there, the wolves had a two-year-old heifer down on her side with her paunch ripped open, and the wolves were eating her insides. She had her head up and was trying to fight them.

In the late fall and early winter, the old female wolf took her pups out every night to teach them how to hunt. Everybody saddled horses in the evening and kept them saddled all night so they would be ready to ride when the cattle started bawling. Many a night was spent running wolves away from the cattle. At about the same time, ranchers were trying to raise some work horse stock by breeding Percheron studs to the little Indian pony mares. Work stock was a good cash flow product, but some of the ranchers in the area never raised a colt for three or four years, or until they got rid of the wolves.

A wolf is a deadly killer. He has a lot more power in his jaws than any dog. A lot of the cattle at that time had no tails. As the wolf pups didn't know how to hunt, they would jump up and grab a cow by the tail right next to the body and bite it right square off.

Tom Berry got some Russian and Irish wolfhounds to hunt wolves, but every time he caught a wolf, the wolf killed two or three of his dogs. One time when he was tracking a wolf in the snow, there were two coyotes following the wolf. From a hill top, Tom saw one of the coyotes get too close to the wolf, and the wolf reached over and killed it with one bite.

THREE TOES AND THE LAST OF THE WOLVES
IN THE BADLANDS AREA

In about 1914 and 1915, the wolves were a big problem in that they were killing lots of livestock. Area ranchers put a bounty on the wolves and hired a wolfer by the name of Fred Hansen, a skilled trapper and hunter. By the spring of 1916 he had gotten all the wolves but one well-known one called Three Toes. Fred had caught him in a trap when he was just a pup and was never able to trap him again.

Three Toes disappeared in the middle of the winter of 1915-16. Fred thought someone might have gotten him or he might have left the country. In March of 1916, Fred saw his tracks, and he had another wolf with him. Fred figured he had gone  somewhere and found him a female. Fred just waited until they denned with pups, along in May, then tracked them down and found the den. Fred got the female and all four pups, but Three Toes got away. During the summer and fall, Three Toes was heard howling, and once in a while a kill was found. In the early fall Three Toes' howl was heard no more.

In April or early May of 1917, Fred, knowing well the sound of Three Toes' howl, heard him howl, and heard another wolf answer him. Fred went to looking for sign and finally about the middle of June found the den. Three Toes had come back with two females, one gray and one red, part dog. Both females had denned together not too far from where Three Toes had denned before. Fred got the two females and nine pups from the den, but Three Toes was not to be found. Three Toes stayed in the area that summer and early fall. You could hear his lonely howl now and then.

Three Toes was a smart old wolf, traveling the ridges where the snow was blowed off so he wouldn't leave any tracks. Nobody was ever able to catch him in a trap after his first encounter with one.

In the early winter of 1917, he wasn't heard of again, and no tracks were seen. Fred Hansen went to work for Tom Berry as a ranch hand. The Berry ranch at that time was located on Black Pipe Creek. There was a big high hill across the creek to the west of the ranch. One early morning in March of 1919, Fred was going down to milk the cow before breakfast, when he heard Three Toes howl from the top of that high hill. Fred went on and milked the cow and saddled his horse, and after breakfast he picked up the track and tracked him over to about the same area where he had denned before. This area is real rough, choppy Badlands with a big Badland wall on the south and east sides, about 14 miles south of Belvidere east of Highway 63. Fred rode up on the wall and jumped Three Toes, and shot him as he ran off the wall.

In the time that Three Toes was gone from 1917 to 1919 he must have been making a big circle looking for another mate, but none was to be found. Three Toes was a smart old wolf, traveling the ridges where the snow was blowed off so he wouldn't leave any tracks. Nobody was ever able to catch him in a trap after his first encounter with one. Three Toes and most wolves were hard to poison. They might go back to a kill about the third night. They would not go up to the kill but just scratch around and howl. Fred said it was very unusual for a wolf to have more than one female and for two females to den together was unheard of.

This is part of the passing of the west and best left in the past. ●

CARNIVAL PRIZE FIGHTER

In the 1930's I stayed in Watertown, South Dakota, for a while. As a young boy I got to hanging around the carnival. I liked the animals and stayed around there most of the time. They also had a boxing ring, and every night there would be plenty of fights. Most of the fights were supposed to be three rounds, and the challenger got one dollar a round. If he wasn't able to stay in a full round he didn't get anything.

The carnival had a big, tough old boy with a big belly that was hard as a rock. He was an old fighter who knew his business. He knew all the dirty tricks of the trade. He'd hit below the belt and if somebody did last a round, he hit them as hard as he could after the bell. I hung around there for about three nights. No one ever lasted a round.

Now in the thirties a dollar was a lot of money, so they had a lot of takers—farm boys, hobos, and anyone else who thought they could stay a round. Now the old prize fighter knew the only way he could keep his job was to not let anybody last a round except when the promoters told him to.

They would pass the hat until they got enough money to start the fight. When the hat came by me, I never seen anything in it but pennies and a few nickels. When they thought they had enough they would start the fight. On about the fourth night when I was watching the fight, I looked over and standing next to me was a big skinny kid with a pair of tennis shoes hanging over his shoulder. Now most everybody else that got in the ring took their shoes off and fought barefooted, so just the sign of the shoes made me think he was something special.

I started talking to him, and he told me he came to get the prize fighter's job. He stood around with me and watched the old prize fighter fight. Then he handed me his shoes and went up and talked to the promoters and got the next fight. He came back over and got his shoes, got in the ring, and started to fight. Right away you could see he knew what he was doing, and you could tell by the look on the old prize fighter's face that he did, too. About halfway through the second round the kid knocked the old prize fighter out.

The kid took his job. I watched him a couple of nights and he was good. I didn't get back to the carnival for a night or two, but I did get back the last day they were to be in town. I went down to the boxing ring to see the kid but he was gone. They had a new carnival prize fighter. ●

CHRISTMAS EVE RIDE

I'd just been back to the Antler Ranch a few days, and Bill Greenough the cow boss wanted to know where I was going for Christmas. I had no relations in the area, so just figured on staying at the ranch. He wanted to know if I'd be willing to go over to a neighboring ranch that had a bunch of Antler steers running on their place. Since they were feeding their cows, they wanted to get rid of the Antler steers pretty bad, so I threw my saddle and bed roll in the back of his pickup and took along some warm winter clothes. There was about five inches of snow on the ground. He drove me over to an old cow camp on the east fork of Pryor Creek. There were a couple of horses there that I'd had in my string last summer, a black horse called Humpy and a bay horse called the Jerkaway Bay. I saddled up the black, even though he did buck, because I figured I had a better chance on him than I did on the Jerkaway Bay. If I got off the bay and wasn't really careful, he'd jerk away and get away, setting me on foot. I got on old Humpy and rode him around the corral until I finally got the hump out of his back. At this time it was about four o'clock in the evening, just beginning to get dusk. Bill said "The ranch is about eight miles northeast of here.

They're expecting you, and you'll be able to see their lights." I rode into their place about six thirty, just as they were done eating supper. They came out and showed me where to put my horses, and took me to the nicest bunk house I'd ever seen. It had a nice big bed in it, and was nice and warm, so I just threw my bed roll down outside, and they took me over to the main house for supper. They had company and a nice big supper. They were part Indian, and awfully nice people, though their name has long since been forgotten.

After supper, they told me they were having a dance in Pryor, Montana that night, and wondered if I wanted to go along. I accepted the invitation gladly. They said to go to the bunk house and look in the closet; there were some shirts hanging in there, and I could take my pick to wear for the night. I went and looked through the shirts, the first snap-button shirts I'd ever seen in my life, and the tag on them said "Made by Rodeo Ben." The shirts belonged to their son, who was off going to school. I picked a yellow corduroy shirt. The shirts were all a little too big, but I just rolled the cuffs back and made them work.

At the dance, they said "There's another kid here from South Dakota that we'd like to have you meet," so we went out in the hallway of that old school to meet him. He was an Indian boy, but he said he wasn't from South Dakota, though his folks were. He had the reputation of being a bronc rider, and we visited quite a while. On the way home the folks I was staying with told me that his family, who were Sioux, came there looking for a place to hide after the Battle of the Little Bighorn. For some reason, there was a small group of Nez Perce Indians on the Crow Indian Reservation around Pryor, Montana who took them in.

I would gather a straight job truck load of steers, then I would call the Antler Ranch, and they would send a truck for them. I gathered three and a half loads of steers, then tied my saddle and bedroll on the truck when I sent out the last load. The ranchers where I stayed said they'd turn my horses loose, and they'd go back to camp on their own. I got back to the Antler Ranch on New Year's Eve. ♠

HOMESTEADERS

In 1913 the government opened the Rosebud Indian Reservation in South Dakota. Mellette County was in the Reservation. Most of the families, when they came in, had a team, a little bit of farm machinery, and a milk cow or two. Some were lucky and got a fairly good piece of land and seemed to do all right. Some of their relatives are still in the area. A lot of them took up homesteads down in the rough Badlands. Most of the homesteads had to be fenced, and the rest of the land was open range. There were quite a few Indian and white ranchers running cattle on this land. They raised a little crop over a period of years, but most of the time not enough to ever get ahead. If a milk cow had a calf and they didn't get it branded, the calf would get out with the range cattle, and they very seldom got it back. Times were hard, and a little free meat was a godsend. Over the years, most of them had sold off what livestock they had, even their team of horses. A lot of them had nothing left on the place but a few chickens. Over the years with drought it really was a hard way to make a living.

In the 1920's and 30's, the majority of the homesteaders were broke. Baxter Berry was one of the ranchers in that area. He rode horseback around to the homesteads and he told me a quarter of land and everything on it would cost 90 dollars; and a half section, 120. He carried cash and quit-claim deeds, and bought land right on the spot. He said that if he stopped at a homestead at dinner time, they always asked him in to eat; most of them never had much, but were willing to share. A lot of them had worked on their little piece of land for 10 or 15 years, and had lost all their money and all their dreams. He said they were so happy to get their hands on the money so they could get out of the country. One of the last homesteaders to leave the Badlands homestead was Ohana Jensen, who lived back in the real rough Badlands with a little bunch of goats, and had dugouts dug back in the banks. He and his wife first settled on a homestead by Horseshoe Butte, and things got way too tough for her, so she left and he moved down into the Badlands.

Some other homesteaders I knew by the name of Malonik settled out on the prairie north of Cottonwood, South Dakota. They came from Austria, and told me they had a nice little farm at the foot of the mountains. The government was going to draft one of the boys, so they came to the United States instead, where they found land for homesteading through a land agent. They got on an immigrant train in New York and came to South Dakota to take over their land. When they got here and saw what they had, three quarters of hardpan and cactus, they had no money to go back, so had to stay. They finally went to work in the section crew on the railroad in order to make a living.

Often when you're out riding checking on cattle, you'd see a pickup driving around; you'd go over and talk to them, and find out it was some of the family looking for where their grandparents had homesteaded. It was hard to find the old places, as generally there was nothing left, because the ranchers rolled up the fences, and the old buildings just rotted away. ●

CASINO

Casino was a bay gelding, mostly Morgan bred. We were up workin' cattle in the Interior, South Dakota country; Frank Walker had a little bay horse that he gave to Baxter Berry. When we trailed home we brought the horse along. He was a bronc, and would try to jump by us and kick whenever I went to saddle him or got off him. He liked to buck, and could do a pretty good job of it. I'd rode him about 10 times when Bax said "I'm just going to give him to you, because nobody else will ride him." I rode him for several years, and he never changed much, except he finally quit kicking at me unless he was sure he'd score.

I was workin' over on the Jones ranch, livin' on a little camp that had about 40 acres around the buildings. Boss called me up on a Sunday and wanted me to help him work a pasture early Monday morning; so I had to get my horses in the corral Sunday so I could leave early Monday morning. I tried every way— coaxing them in with grain, and they'd have no part of that; then I tried to corral them, but that didn't work either. We went around and around the little trap. There was a yard fence around the house with two gates in it. They got to going through the yard, through one gate and then the other, so I let them do it several times, then shut the one gate. They went into the yard and I shut the other gate on them, and had them, but I still couldn't catch Casino. I finally caught the other little horse I called Ginger, a nice little horse but would buck with me too if I didn't warm him up pretty good; so I saddled him up and rode him around quite a little. Finally I went over to the yard, tied the rope to the saddle horn, and roped Casino. In the yard was an old 32-volt wind charger that had several guy wires on it; when I roped Casino, he ran around one of the guy wires and got all tangled up. I thought we were going to jerk the wind charger down, all the racket we made. My wife was in the house taking a nap, and all

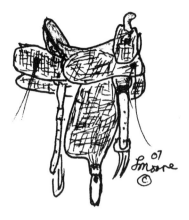

the noise brought her right out of the house, thinking the house was caving in. We finally got Casino untangled and put him in the corral. Out behind the corral was a stack yard with one big haystack in it. I opened the gate so he could go out in there for the night.

The next morning I went out to catch Casino, and I couldn't get him in the corral, as he kept running around that big stack, and wouldn't go in the corral gate. This was about four o'clock in the morning; I went over to the house and got Jean, my wife, out of bed to help me. I told her "You stand here between the haystack and the gate (which wasn't a very big area), and when he comes around the haystack, wave your arms and turn him into the corral gate." I brought him around the stack and she tried turning him into the corral gate; he just laid his ears back, and took a run at her, strikin'. She got out of the way, and with a few very choice words for me and the horse, went back to bed. I kept after him until he finally went into the corral; catchin' him and saddlin' him was quite an ordeal. I got on him and made it to the pasture on time. Casino was mad and determined not to work that day, but I guess I was madder and more determined!

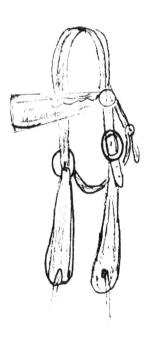

SHORTY

Shorty was a little sorrel horse that I bought in Philip, South Dakota in about 1955. I believe he was about three years old, and I was looking for that kind of horse, as I had three little kids and one on the way, and I thought he just might work for them. He turned out to be real gentle, and it wasn't long before the kids could all ride him. My oldest boy started riding Shorty the four miles to school when he was in the first grade. If he fell off, Shorty would just stop and stand there until Casey could get back on. It wasn't long until I had three kids going to school, two riding Shorty and one on a Palomino horse we had, called Timpsela. Shorty got so he didn't mind the kids riding him at all, but if I saddled him to ride him, he'd buck every time. We moved to a little town called Cottonwood, South Dakota when my youngest boy, Mike, was about four years old. He had to wait until Shorty put his head down to graze, then he'd jump on his neck and kick him with his heels

until Shorty would throw his head up. Then Mike would slide down his neck and get on his back. He made a trip around town every morning, riding bareback, and always carried his security blanket in front of him on old Shorty. He stopped in front of every house in town, and just sat on his horse until one of the ladies would bring him a cookie or something. Everybody got a big kick out of him, as he wouldn't hardly talk.

Shorty was a pretty good little race horse, as we raced him quite a lot for 220 yards. Casey, my oldest boy, was 10 or 11 then, and rode him bareback with a handful of mane, and would generally be across the finish line before most of the other horses got started.

Shorty was getting old, so I run onto a fellow by the name of Theodore Kjerstad who lived north of Quinn, South Dakota that had some little kids. I sold him the horse for $60 and told him "When you get done with him, call me. I'll give you your $60 back, and come and get the horse." I had moved back to the Berry ranch when they offered me the job of managing it. I got a call one day, so went up and got the horse, just pensioned him and turned him out to pasture. He got big and fat, and ran there for several years.

THE HUNTING PARTY

(As told by my great granddad to my uncle.)

Right after the Civil War, Philip Hunter moved from Tennessee to southern Iowa. He homesteaded on a farm and done enough farming to feed his family. Generally in early fall he would come West into South Dakota and the surrounding area. He was a hunter and a trapper. When he got enough hides and furs to sell he would go back to Iowa.

On one of his trips West he throwed in with a hunting party of Sioux Indians. They were traveling somewhere east of the Black Hills on

the edge of the Badlands. Traveling along a creek they went into the head of a big draw and run onto a big grizzly bear. The Indians were mostly all armed with bows and arrows. Being mounted horseback, they rode by on both sides and finally managed to shoot him with some arrows. Now this old bear was bawling and charging and finally ran down the creek and up a draw into a big hole. Philip had a gun but didn't get off a shot.

The Indians built a fire out in front of the hole far enough away so they could get away if the bear did come out. They got out their pipe and smoked and made medicine. They wanted to give the bear time to die or stiffen up. A young man volunteered to go in after the bear.

After quite some time they decided it was time to go after the bear. The young man took a cedar torch and his lance. The rest of the Indians and Philip gathered up on each side of the hole. All of a sudden the bear went to growling and bawling. The young man came running out of the hole with the bear right on his heels. He had buried the lance in the bear. The Indians shot arrows at the bear, but Philip downed the bear with his gun. They took the bear claws. The young man who went into the hole after the bear got most of the claws. ◑

LOAD OF HAY

During the drought of 1936 I was eight years old. I was working for my room and board for some German farmers down around Norris, South Dakota. We were stacking thistles. We would go out along the fence lines where they had blown into the fences. There weren't a whole lot of them as some of the fences were covered with sand. We would follow the fences with hay rack and pitchforks and throw the thistles in the rack, haul them in and sack them. One of my jobs was to tromp on them. Which means you would have to jump down on them and tromp them down with your feet. It was hot and dry and those thistles were damn sticky.

We were stackin' one morning when a couple of Indian men pulled up with the nicest load of green hay you ever saw. They were asking a dollar for that load of hay. Nobody around there had a dollar. So they went on down the road. Now this was South of Norris which was generally good farmland. I kept watching them as they went from place to place. They finally went over a hill out of sight. Along late that evening they came back by with an empty rack.

In this day of big machinery and lots of dollars, I have often thought about it. A good team of horses and a mower with a five foot bar can mow five acres a day. They had a little team of Indian ponies that could only pull a four foot bar. Then they had to rake the hay, bunch it, and pitch it on a little rack, and then spend a day selling it. I think it took three days of work for 50 cents. ♠

THE LANTERN GLOBE

When I got out of the Marines, I got a job working for Lee Yokum. We were building some tourist cabins up by Hill City, South Dakota. I believe those cabins are still there to this day. Lee was an old man and quite a character. He had been an old cowboy that had been on some of the early roundups. He talked like he had worked mostly in Nebraska and Wyoming. He worked on several big cow and horse outfits including the CBC horse outfit.

Working for one of the outfits in Nebraska the old wagon boss took a liking to Lee and gave him his old six-shooter. It was an old single action Colt 45 with bone handles on it. We were looking it over and took the handles off and under the handles we found three notches filed in it. The old wagon boss had been from Missouri and according to Lee never talked much about his life.

Lee was working for this same old wagon boss. The wagon was camped out south of Edgemont, South Dakota. All the cowboys were figuring on going to town for the 4th of July, except the wagon boss and the cook. All the younger boys were catching their broncy horses to ride to town to show off. Lee had a blue roan horse in his string that was real broncy and bad to buck. When Lee got on him in camp everybody was watching including the wagon boss and the cook. The horse blew up, bucked all over with Lee just barely making the ride pulling everything he could just to stay on. When the horse got done the wagon boss said, "Lee, the cook wants you to bring a lantern globe back to camp with you." So the cowboys went to town and stayed three or four days and celebrated the 4th of July.

Now Lee wasn't one to let any kind of a challenge go by. So he had to figure out how to get the lantern globe home. There wasn't much of any way to carry it without it getting broke. They finally figured out how to do it. They threw the blue horse down, run the lantern globe up his tail, covered it as good as they could and tied a knot in the end of his tail. He delivered the lantern globe back to camp in fine shape.

♠

POOL WAGON

In the 1920's in the area south of Belvidere, South Dakota, they operated what they called the Pool Wagon. The ranchers in that area got together and put up money to put an outfit together so they could gather and work their cattle, since none of the ranchers had enough cattle to work them on their own, and it was all open range. Most of the country they worked was on the Rosebud Indian Reservation in South Dakota. Indians and whites worked together part of the time. Some of those in the pool were Hans Thode, Willie Rooks, Corny Utterback, Pettijohns, and Tom Berry. As the wagon moved around the country working cattle, the rancher who was most acquainted with that area became wagon boss.

In 1928, the wagon started out over in the area of the Berry Ranch. Just southwest of where the Berry house is now was a big spring. It had been an old Indian campground for years, and now the cowboys

 camped there as they came through the country. Earl Thode was a young man and riding a bunch of broncs. He got on a gray horse there one morning that really bucked hard. All the old timers said nobody could ride him but Earl Thode. When he finally stopped bucking, Earl had his spurs locked in the cinch so hard he couldn't get them out, so Tom Berry and Hans Thode (Earl's dad) rode up on each side of the horse and snugged him up, and loosened Earl's cinch so he could get his spurs out. At that time in this country, the custom was to buckle your spurs on the inside; ever after that, Earl buckled his spurs on the outside, so he could get at them if he needed to. That fall, Earl went to Frontier Days Rodeo in White River, South Dakota and won the bronc riding; that started his career to becoming a world champion.

Another member of the pool was Corny Utterback, who got that nickname from the Indians because he smoked a corncob pipe. He

married a half French-half Indian woman, who had two sisters married to white men, and one sister married to Chief Crazy Horse.

Corny branded an anvil brand on both sides, so they'd brand the calf on one side, roll him over, and brand him on the other. Corny had quite a little money, which he had buried in the yard around his house. He started quite a few cowboys in business, as he loaned that money out. They'd talk over the business in the house, and if they decided to loan him the money, his wife would leave the house and come back with a canful of money.

Another member was Willie Rooks, who ran a lot of horses also. He put big herds of horses together, and trailed them south into Nebraska and Colorado, where he sold them. It seems one time he had some horses that didn't belong to him, and I think he served some time in the penitentiary. Tom Berry told me that the day Willie was to get out of the pen, he was coming into Belvidere by train. Family and

everybody went to Belvidere to meet him, but he never showed up because he stayed at the pen to play his fiddle for a dance.

Charlie Larson as a kid came up from Missouri and worked for the Rosebud Sioux tribe as a cowboy, and went with their roundup wagon. The Indians had quite a few cattle, all of them branded with their own brand, plus a government brand ID on the right hip. Pretty near all the Indian cowboys brought their families with them, so there'd be the roundup wagon and 15-20 Teoly wagons with their families and a couple hundred head of horses. Charlie said they pow-wowed about every night and butchered every day, and it didn't make any difference to them whose cow they butchered. If she was fat and dry, and that Indian had only that one cow, that's still the one they butchered.

Another member of the pool was Hans Thode, who had a place down on the White River.

Mrs. Thode ran a road house, and anyone who was there at mealtime got fed, whether they could pay for it or not. She also raised nine kids. Hans was a rugged character, as he and some Wyoming cowboys team-roped Grizzly bears just for sport. Most oldtimers said he was a better bronc rider than his son Earl. Charlie Larson had worked for Hans quite a lot as a kid. A horse would be bucking him and about to throw him off when Hans would ride up and jump on behind and hold him on

When the pool wagon got back around Belvidere, Hans Thode became the wagon boss. They camped at a place south of Belvidere called Jack Springs. The cowboys all decided to go to town, and it must have been quite a party; some of them decided to solve their problems and got to fighting. The Indian policeman had the only gun, and Tom Berry and Hans Thode talked him out of it. I think maybe the Indians got the worst of it, as they had more hair to get a hold of. The next morning some of them wouldn't get out of bed, so Hans just cut their saddle horses out and left them lying in their beds on the prairie. In a couple of days they caught up with the wagon, and everything went pretty much back to normal.

STANDING TALL

The spring I was 14, I thought I was quite a cowboy, as I had broke a few Shetland ponies and such. Burrell Phipps had a couple of two year old colts. I sure wanted to ride them. I finally talked Bax into letting me break them to ride, so I went down to Burrel's to do it.

The colts had been broke to lead and were fairly gentle. Burrel and I caught one, tied up a hind leg, sacked him out, and put hobbles on him. Bax had gotten me a nice little EC saddle, but it weighed about as much as I did. When I finally got it up high enough to put on the colt's back and dropped it on him, he jumped by me and kicked me in the belly. He knocked all the wind out of me and flattened me. Burrel drug me over to the side of the corral and saddled the colt. Burrel was building a log barn at the time, and left to go work on it, so just left the colt saddled in the corral.

I laid there and looked at the colt. I was sick and scared. I couldn't even saddle him......how was I going to ride him? At that time, at that age, the worst thing that you could have told me was that I couldn't make a cowboy. About that time, Paul Berry came along. He took one look at me, walked over and caught the colt, gathered up the reins and just stepped up on him. The bolt blew up, went to bucking and bucked all over the corral.

Paul stood about six foot tall, and I was under four feet. When the colt blew up, Paul stood up in the stirrups, his knees were even with the seat of my saddle, but he rode him good. When the colt quit bucking, Paul got off, patted him on the neck and chuckled a little and went to help Burrel. It sure made me feel good and I went on and got the colt rode.

Paul Berry was a hero that day, and to me, he still is. ●

TRAILING HORSES

In the fall of 1949 Gib Peck and I were working on the Berry Double X Ranch. Baxter send us over to help Jones at Midland, South Dakota. Jones at that time ran a lot of cattle out on summer pastures and trailed them home in the fall. The Jones ranch was owned by the great old timer Tom Jones. Tom had a thousand of steers up North of Midland, close to the Cheyenne River on the Foley place. Tom said, "I want you to trail our saddle horses up there and we'll meet you up there with the wagon." He said, "Now I've made a deal for you boys to stay overnight with Jim Nelson." I didn't know where Nelsons lived but Gib had been up there before and had a pretty good idea where he lived. Jim's was about 30 or 35 miles from the ranch and about halfway to the Foley place.

We trailed along pretty well and got in to the Nelson place in early evening. There was nobody home. We were hungry as we had had no dinner and were tired from the long ride. We looked around and found a little pasture where we could turn our horses. Gib tied his rope to the horn of his saddle, rode through the horses and caught two night horses, two loops, two horses. Gib was an excellent sneak roper.

We sat around for a while, I said to Gib, "Let's go up and set in the house." Gib said, "Oh, we can't do that." Gib was part Indian. "When they come home and see me setting in the house they will think that I am some Mexican outlaw."

So we stayed around the barn. The hay mow had some hay in it. I went up there and rolled up in my slicker and went to sleep. About four o'clock in the morning the Nelsons got home. They cooked up a big breakfast and we sure filled up on it. We caught our night horses and saddled up and trailed on up to the Foley place. We got in there about five o'clock in the afternoon. Now the wagon wasn't there yet. The wagon Jones used was a pickup with a mess box on the back. We used a tent for cooking and sleeping. We caught a couple of night horses and finally Tom and about four cowboys showed up. They had a cook by the name of Harry Clinton and he sure cooked up a good supper. We rolled out our beds and they sure felt good. ♠

WHITESIDES

In the late 1920's my folks bought a meat market in Norris, South Dakota. Norris at that time was quite a town. It had a bank, cream station, gas station, and two or three stores. The main store was the Outlaw Trading Post. There weren't many cars but there were still many teams of horses that were used.

My folks butchered three times a week to keep everybody in meat. There were lots of homesteaders. Being on the Rosebud Indian Reservation there was a lot of Indian trade also. On the days they butchered they took a soupbone, put an onion and a potato in with it, and wrapped it in newspaper. They called it a poke. It was then put it in a tub and they gave them away to whoever wanted them.

My dad was an old cowboy and horseman. One day some people came into town driving a team of horses. In that team was a black and white spotted horse. They stopped in front of the Outlaw Trading Post went in and sold their cream and bought some groceries. When they went to leave, the old black and white horse balked on them and wouldn't budge. They whipped and beat on him. My dad couldn't stand to see the horse whipped so he bought the horse. My dad was also Deputy Sheriff. He

gave them a fair price, they didn't argue much and he had them unhook the horse right away. Now this horse had quite a reputation in that area. He was mean and bucked real hard.

Berry's had a big ranch just north of Norris in the Badlands. My dad sent the horse up there as he was sick and couldn't ride anymore. Berry turned the horse out and let him freshen up. Then Baxter Berry got him in and went to riding him.

Bax had some wild horses running north of the ranch. There weren't many fences in the country then. The stock just run wherever they wanted to. Bax had two mares with two colts running on them with this bunch of wild horses. These horses were running just south of where the Interstate runs now between Kadoka and Belvidere. There are three or four white looking flat topped buttes right there. That's approximately 20 miles across country up there from the ranch. Bax saddled up and rode old Whitesides and run those horses down. He cut out the two mares and yearling colts and trailed them back to the ranch. It was a 40 mile ride. It is hard telling how much farther he rode to run them down.

Old Whitesides wasn't nice or pretty but you could ride him to the end of the world and back and still be horseback.

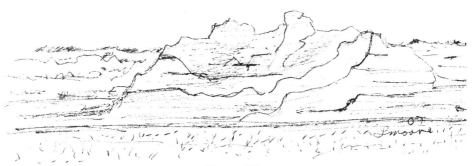

STOPPIN' THE RUNAWAY

The Berry Ranch on the Rosebud Indian Reservation in South Dakota put up a lot of hay when it was rainin' in the 40's. It was all done with horses, and pretty near all the help were Indians. They had a big camp just west of the ranch on the flats, with about 24-25 government-issue tents set up. About 25 went to work every day. We ran seven horse mowers, two rakes, a bull sweep outfit (four horses hooked to a big hay sweep), and seven hayracks, one man with a pitchfork on each hayrack. They hauled six loads a day apiece.

I was a horse wrangler, wrangled horses every morning about four o'clock, and again at noon. I generally rode a bronc. It was quite a sight to watch the Indian boys catch horses in the morning, as they all made fun and had a sense of humor. The only horses we changed at noon were the mowing teams. Pretty near all were good hands and done a good job. As Baxter told them, "If you walk very far off from your team, be sure and unhook them from whatever you were pulling, and tie up your lines." That way, if a team ran away, they just ran away with the harness. The men all followed those orders real good. The mowers and the bull sweep crew generally started around seven in the morning, and went most of the day. The hayracks started rolling about five, to finish before the heat of the day, because pitching hay was hard work; as soon as they hauled six loads of hay, they could quit for the day. Most of the stacks were put up in 100-ton stacks, rolled up with ropes. Every hayrack had a rope sling in it; we'd back up to the stack, tie the sling ropes to the stack ropes, hook the team to a big bull rope and pull the load up on the stack. There were three men to each stack, two on the stack, and one tying ropes. I was 15 years old at the time, and one of my jobs was tying ropes. We could put up a lot of hay in a day.

One of the Indians working there was Henry Medicine Blanket. Bax let him have a big gray team to use, as at that time a team was transportation, and they used them for hauling wood and other things. Bax loaned out several teams to Indians since at that time, there weren't a lot of cars in our country. The big gray team were bad to run

away. Henry came in to the stack one day and backed up to roll off his hay. I tied the ropes, and Henry went back and pulled his load off, brought his team back and was going to hook them onto his hayrack, when the team broke and ran before he got them hooked up. For some reason, the team turned and ran straight back toward the hayrack. I was standing right next to Tom Berry. As the team came by, Tom reached out and grabbed a neck yoke, and it went over the head and dropped one of the horses just like you'd shot him with a cannon. I looked over at old Henry; his eyes were bigger than his hat. He didn't think Tom could move that fast, and I didn't either. The team did pretty good after that for a few days. ●

CROOKED LEGGED BROWN

Two or three of us were riding back to camp one day after working a little bunch of cattle. We got to visiting about our horses, and I told the other two cowboys that I had my horse ridin' pretty good, that I could just jump him out and turn a cow. I decided to show them, so I spurred him a little bit, and he jumped out and went to bucking. They thought it was real funny, and went to laughing. Then when we got to camp, they had to tell Bill Greenough, the cow boss.

Bill didn't think it was funny at all. He said, "If he wants to spur one, I've got one in the cavvy that he won't need to spur." The next morning, Bill caught the crooked legged brown for me. He was big and snorty, and I guess you could call him a snake. It wasn't easy to get him saddled, and I thought when I did, he'd blow up and buck, but all he did was hump around. I led him around in a circle for a while, trying to limber him up, and finally got him around to where I could get on. Most of their bad horses were spoiled to get on, but he finally let me on him. It was just like settin' on a keg of dynamite! He didn't buck right away, but rode about a 100 yards, and all the hands headed the same way to go on circle when he finally blowed. Talk about going into the air! I don't believe I'd ever been that high in the air on a horse in my life, and I can say now that I was scared. He didn't have a whole lot of snap to him in the air, and I rode him all right. I went on a little further, and Bill turned me on circle by myself, and it was a short circle—five or six miles—and the further we went, the broncer he got, both ears laid flat, and watching every move I made. I got back to camp without him bucking again, and I was sure glad to get off. I never rode the horse again, and I never saw anyone else ride him. We had packed him in the cavvy all summer, and he was only rode once. I think they had the horse laying back, just laying for somebody who thought he was a bronc rider. ●

COMING HOME

In the spring of 1945, I was working for the Bird Head Ranch in Wyoming. There was an old fellow there doing the chore work on the ranch whose son came home from the Marines. He'd been over in the South Pacific and come home from the war because he had a bad case of Malaria. The Bird Head had a bunch of broncs they were trying to get broke. Three or four different cowboys had tried them and give up and had them pretty badly spoiled. I can't remember this veteran's name, but he took on the job of breaking them to ride, and got along good except about every week or 10 days, Malaria would come back on him, and he'd get sick and weak. It'd take him a week or so to get over that, but he finally got the broncs broke.

Then I decided I'd like to work for the Antlers, as they were pulling out their roundup wagon, and I wanted to go. That fall, and along in the winter—I believe after the first of the year—the boss ran in about 20 head of broncs that needed to be broke to ride. About that time, he hired another Marine veteran that they called Brownie. He had also been somewhere in the South Pacific, and had caught a bunch of shrapnel, most of it from his waist down. He had scars all over his backside and down his legs, with part of his penis blown off, and his testicles. About once a month, he'd have to go to Billings Montana to the veterans' hospital, as that shrapnel kept working out to his skin, and had to be cut out. He was a good hand, could ride about anything, but finally got to drinking so bad that the boss had to let him go.

When Frank was cow boss, he would try to hire any wounded veteran that came along. At one time he hired two veterans, one that had a left leg blown off, and the other with his right leg blown off. They could ride a horse all right, but had a lot of trouble getting on, as they couldn't throw that wooden leg over the cantle of the saddle. One had to get on the right side of a horse instead of the left side, so Frank and the boys worked with some old gentle horses and got them so he could get on the right side. Neither one of the boys stayed very long, for even the short rides were too painful for them, and they finally quit, but it wasn't for the lack of trying. ●

COWBOYS

In western South Dakota there are a lot of good cowboys, pretty much from the Missouri River to the Black Hills. In this country, there were a lot of bad horses that were rode and used. The earlier day cowboys seemed to take a lot of pride in how tough a horse they could ride and get their work done. I believe it's a thing of the past, as you don't see much of that anymore.

I grew up on the Double X Ranch owned by Tom and Baxter Berry, where riding broncs was the norm. It just seems to me that that was about the only kind of horse there was to ride. I raised two boys of my own, named Casey and Mike, and another boy the same age as Mike, whose name was Dave Krossert; these boys grew up riding colts and broncs, and by the time they were 16 or 17, they could ride about anything and still get their work done. Casey was the best rider, and Mike the best roper. Casey rode buckin' horses for a while, but didn't draw very good, so I talked him out of it, as he roped pretty good too; a bad calf might take him out of the money, but it wasn't going to break his leg! We were running a big ranch, and I needed his help. Mike rode barebacks in high school and placed fourth in the finals at New Underwood. Dave Krossert was a calf roper, and placed third in the finals.

I traded for some old bucking horses that had quit bucking; the boys took and rode them, and most of them made good circle horses. Don Height traded me a gray horse that he said was broke to ride, that when he bought Norvel Cooper's horses, they were riding that horse.

I took the horse home, got on him and rode him a few times, and I could tell he was a cowboy's horse. I put him in Casey's string, and he rode him some; then that fall, Mike started riding him.

For Baxter Berry, who owned the ranch, working off the big beef steers was the highlight of his years. We shipped them in late summer, generally working them in mid-August. We'd bunch about 2500 beef steers on a big flat we called the Brown Table so we could work off about a 1000 head to ship. The women and spectators came out in cars and brought us some lunch; we ate our lunch and we set up a rope corral to change horses. Mike caught the gray horse and saddled him up; that horse blew up and went to buckin', bucked around and threw Mike off, bucked through the rope corral, and scattered our horses. When we finally got everything back under control and penned the horses in the rope corral again, Mike caught Old Gray, cinched his saddle down, and got on. Burrell Phipps rode right up alongside of Mike and helped him get by him. Baxter Berry was too crippled up to help work the steers, so was standing there watching, and he said, "Well, there's one thing about it, boys: this is still a cow outfit!"

When they sold the ranch, I sold that gray horse to Johnny Holloway, who had a rodeo outfit and was putting on SDRA rodeos. Matt Mattlick was riding buckin' horses at this time; he said if you drew the gray horse (whom they'd named the Gray Ghost) and could stay on, you were in the money.

ROPERS

In the 1930's, there weren't many ropers around. Most of the people were homesteaders and farmers, and didn't know how to rope, and a lot of them didn't even ride horseback. Quite a few of them had put little herds of cattle together, maybe 50 or 60 cows; they found out that ropin' the calves or "healing them", as it was called, made it a lot easier to brand them. Stan Callen, Alex Whipple, and Charlie Larson were old time cowboys who roped hundreds of calves for the homesteaders every spring. Now these oldtimers used what was called a grass rope, nothing like the ropes we have today. If the weather got damp, the rope got so stiff you could hardly use it; and if

> **Quite a few of them had put little herds of cattle together, maybe 50 or 60 cows; they found out that ropin' the calves or "healing them", as it was called, made it a lot easier to brand them.**

it was hot and dry, it got so limp you could hardly build a loop. These oldtimers tied the rope to the horn and drug calves on quite a lot more rope than they do today. Healing calves with one of those old limp ropes was not an easy thing. Another roper that I knew of was Gib Valandry. Gib was quite a roper, and used a big loop. He could ride into a herd of cattle and threw that big Sunday loop out clear to the end of his rope and catch what he wanted. It was called "sneak roping." Everything was roped without running it, as a lot less stress on the cattle. Gib liked to rope a cow around the neck and pick up one front leg so he didn't choke her. It was a beautiful thing to watch, that big lazy loop settling around a cow's head. Gib carried about a 35 foot grass rope.

Another great roper was Albert Whipple, who carried about a 40 foot rope that he would stretch up and singe the fuzz off of it; then he would wax it. Albert was an artist. I saw him rope a lot of cattle, and never miss a loop.

These ropes broke pretty easy, generally at the hondo, and they'd just tie a new hondo in it, and keep using it until it got too short.

Other good calf healers that I knew were Paul Brunch, Baxter Berry and Burrell Phipps; they would rope calves in the fall until their arm was completely worn out. They were more on the modern concept, as they had rubber on their saddle horn, and dallied.

One of the best ropers I've ever seen, I believe, is Chuck Holloway. You will see him pickin' up broncs at rodeos; he can throw about any kind of loop, and he does it with his left hand.

VETAL

In the spring of 1942, it was wet and rainy, and looked like it was going to be a good hay year. The Berry Ranch was looking forward to putting up a lot of hay, so they traded for a bunch of three-and-four-year-old draft colts, which needed to be broke to drive. They had a township leased south and east of the home place (which was south of Belvidere, South Dakota). On that lease was a camp they called the Rum Camp, and they needed to build a dam there. They had a good cowboy living on that camp by the name of Gib Valandry, and his father, Vetal, lived with him. I think Vetal was 71 years old at the time. His folks had been in on the Battle of the Little Bighorn; his mother was half French and half Indian, and after the battle, made the run to Canada. Vetal's mother met a Frenchman in Canada, and Vetal was born sometime later in Canada. When the family decided to come back to South Dakota, Vetal was a baby. Vetal later settled down along the Nebraska line, an area noted for its grass and lots of water; he ranched there for several years. There's a little town down Highway 18 east of Martin named for him.

"One day Vetal got mad and started hollering at him in Indian; when he did that, all the other teams came to a stop, and they all listened, then went to laughing."

When the 1930's came, Vetal went to work for the WPA, and became what they call "dump boss" on the dams. After getting the horses broke to drive, we moved over to the Rum Camp and started moving dirt, and made Vetal dump boss. We had an entire Indian crew. We ran six four-horse frisnos and a four-horse team plowing. The Indian teamsters, when they pulled in to dump, Vetal would talk to them in English, and they would answer back in Indian. They were always trying to get him to talk in Indian, but Vetal wouldn't do it. They kept telling me, "He's just like us." We had an old Indian working for us by the name of Pokin Horn, and he didn't understand English very well. One day Vetal got mad and started hollering at him in Indian; when he did that, all the other teams came to a stop, and they all listened, then went to laughing. This was the only time I heard him talk Indian.

Vetal went to work for Bax that summer, mowing hay. Bax loaned him a paint team called Slim and Colonel, and a little mountain buggy. He went all different places mowing hay; he'd throw his bed and war bag in the back, and would go wherever they had some hay to mow. When fall came, Vetal only drew a little of his wages. He said, "Baxter, you buy me some steers with the rest of that money, and run them until I die; then sell them to pay my funeral expenses." He moved out to Idaho to stay with his daughter, and when he died, Baxter sold some five-year-old steers and sent them the money. Vetal had several grandkids; they all became teachers or stockmen, and one retired from the US Army as a full Colonel. I guess you could say they are a genuine American family. ●

He said, "Baxter, you buy me some steers with the rest of that money, and run them until I die; then sell them to pay my funeral expenses."

HOLLOWAY RODEO COMPANY

In the 1970's, Holloway's probably had 90 percent of the South Dakota Rodeo Association rodeos. They had a lot of good stock and put on a wild rodeo. Casey and I were going to quite a few SDRA rodeos at that time. When we pulled into Lemmon South Dakota for the "Boss Cowman Rodeo", we drove down to the arena, looked over, and here was little Chuck Holloway—at that time about three years old, I'd guess—standing in front of a loading chute, and a big semi backing up to the chute. Casey jumped out, went over and grabbed Chuck, and pulled him away from behind the truck. The Holloway family were all working at putting on the rodeo, and if they turned their back, little Chuck was gone, and they might find him about anywhere.

Here was little Chuck Holloway—at that time about three years old, I'd guess—standing in front of a loading chute, and a big semi backing up to the chute.

The rodeo went along real smooth with Dick Ward doing the announcing. We got down close to bull riding time, after one section of team roping. A couple of ropers in tie down team roping ran their steer about three quarters the length of the arena, roped him, and stretched him out on the ground. In tie down team roping, your rope was tied to the saddle horn, and the other end on the steer; the header would jump off, run over and tie a rope around the two hind legs of the steer.

While all this was going on, they were loading bulls into the chute. About the time the header jumped off to go tie up the steer, an old black part Highland bull they called Satan tore the gate off his chute, and out he come; he saw the roper going down to tie the steer, and charged him. The header ran back to his horse and got on; Satan went over and hooked the downed steer for a while, then turned and ran for the arena fence, jumping it out in front of the grandstand.

People ran to the top of the grandstand and scattered all over. John Holloway and John Miller were mounted up, doing the job as pickup men in the arena. They rode out as quick as they could and got old Satan roped, and finally with the help of quite a few other hands, got old Satan back in a pen. I think the bull rider was real thankful he got a different draw.

In the next section of team roping, we had another wreck. Bruce Goodman and Jerry Simons from up Zeona way roped a steer and got him down. I don't believe they placed in the money. When they let the steer up, Jerry was sitting on his horse with about 12 feet of rope laying on the ground with a little loop in it about four inches wide. A girl about 14 or 15 was cleaning the arena of stock they'd just roped; when she ran by to get the steer, her horse stuck his hind foot in the little loop laying on the ground, and when it tightened up, things really began to happen. It jerked her horse down, threw her right over her horse's head, and jerked Jerry's horse down too, and things got pretty wild for a while. Somebody finally got the rope cut, and it didn't seem like anybody really got hurt. Casey was in the calf roping, and Casey and I in the team roping; I don't think we placed in either event. This was just the way one Holloway rodeo went. They were always wild, wooly, and plenty Western, and you sure got your money's worth.

It jerked her horse down, threw her right over her horse's head, and jerked Jerry's horse down too, and things got pretty wild for a while.

MY MODEL A PICKUP

In late fall of 1948, I bought an old pickup. I'd never been around cars before, and didn't know a thing about them. The old pickup seemed to have a mind of its own, and if it did start, I'd go a little ways sometimes and the lights would go out. It had all kinds of little tricks, and I couldn't keep up with most of them.

Stan Anderson was going to high school in White River, South Dakota, and decided to ride up and spend the weekend with me at the Berry Ranch. Along toward evening we decided to go in to Norris and take in the New Year's dance. It was cold, getting down around twenty below zero, and 15 miles into Norris, so we decided to try the old pickup instead of riding horseback. Luckily, we got it started and filled it full of water, and went to Norris. Norris wasn't much of a town anymore, but still had a gas station. Someone said we'd better go down and put alcohol in it, so I drove it down and we drained part of the water out, and filled it with alcohol. Then I ran it quite a while to let it mix up good so it wouldn't freeze.

We went up to the dance hall, parked the pickup, looked around, and got ready to go into the hall. There were several teams tied up around, also some saddle horses, and a few cars quite a lot better than mine. The dance was in a big old building with a big stove in one corner and

a big pile of coats in another corner. Under the coats and clothes was stashed a few bottles of whiskey. Drinking wasn't allowed in the hall, but as cold as it was, people were pretty sneaky, and took a drink every so often. Most of the time, everyone would just go outside to take a drink; but that night was so cold, the only time people went outside was to watch a fight. After quite a lot of dancing, everybody was going good to a little band called "The Gumbo Lilies". Lots of different players played with The Gumbo Lilies, so you never knew what would happen; they might be playing four different tunes at the same time, and everybody was having a good time. The piano player got too drunk to stay on the stool, so he just laid on the floor, his shoes off, and his feet up on the stool, trying to play the keys with his feet. About 1:30, they shut the dance down, and everybody started for home. Stan and I went out, and Stan got into the old pickup, while I set the spark and gave it a crank, and to my amazement, it started right up. We got about four miles out of Norris when it got to steaming so bad we couldn't see the road. We had no idea what was wrong with it, so we just kept going. We rolled the windows down and stuck

our heads out in order to see the road. I can still remember trying to see the road and hearing the tug chains rattle on harnesses as teams trotted up the road ditch. We got just to the gate going into the ranch when the pickup quit, so we headed for the bunk house. Berry's main house had burned down a couple years before, and they hadn't rebuilt, so they lived in a little old cold house, and I slept in the bunk house, which was even worse. Stan and I went to bed in the roundup bed, and I told him to take all his clothes to bed with him; and if his feet sweat, to take his boots to bed with him, or they'd be froze solid in the morning. He left his boots out, and they were froze stiff in the morning. He had a terrible time getting them on, and nearly made us late for breakfast. After breakfast, Stan said, "It's too damn cold around here for me," and he saddled up and went home. ●

THE TOWN BRONC RIDER

In the late 30's and early 40's the Double X ranch had well over a hundred head of mares. They had been raising and selling quite a few to the remount service. In 1942 they had a lot of three year old colts to break. Baxter and his wife took a little trip up the Black Hills Roundup at Belle Fourche. Now Bax was kind of looking for somebody to help break these colts. He run on to a cowboy by the name of Rod Kelly.

Now Rod had won some day money in the bronc riding at Belle Fourche. So Bax hired him to come down to the ranch and help break those colts. They started riding these colts and Rod was getting bucked off quite a little. Now Rod didn't like to get a hold of the saddle horn. Bax told him to get a hold of the horn when you need it so you can stay on and ride them. Rod finally went to pullin' leather and got most of them rode.

Now in this bunch of horses there was two that they couldn't ride. Bax was used to riding bad horses and would ride anything that grew hair. They took turns trying to ride them, then decided they needed to do

something different. Now the ranch had a big lease down on the Little White River toward Rosebud. There was a salty cowboy working down there. So Tom Berry, Bax's dad, got in the car and went down to get him. Louis was a salty cowboy and top bronc rider. I don't believe Louis ever rode a horse out of a chute. By this time they had named those two broncs. They called one Pin Ears and the other was Slim Jim.

Louis saddled up Slim Jim first, got on him, they opened the corral gate. Slim Jim took a run at Louis out the gate, blowed up and bucked down over a badland canyon just north of the corral throwing Louis saddle and all. They saddled him up again and Louis got on. Slim Jim bucked as hard as he could with Louis riding him and spurring him every jump. Louis rode these two horses five or six times and then had to got back down and take care of his lease. Rod and Bax rode the colts a while and then started into their fall cattle work.

The first morning out Rod was riding a gentle horse. He told Bax that it was so dark when he was catching horses he couldn't find one. The next morning was the same thing. Baxter asked how come he wasn't riding a colt. Rod said he had had enough of those SOB's. "Better just take me to town."

The next fall Bax got a little white envelope from Nevada. All that was in the envelope was a newspaper clipping. It said Rod Kelly, Nevada State Bronc Riding Champion. Bax got one of those clippings three years in a row.

SLIM JIM AND PIN EARS

They were broncs that were in the bunch of horses that Rod Kelly and Baxter Berry were breakin' to ride. The horses bucked hard, and just wouldn't quit, so the next spring Berry sent these two broncs over to Connie Seidler and Lawrence Grimes who were breakin' a bunch of colts at Connie's dad's place right on the west edge of Red Stone Basin. I don't know how they got along, but they finally turned the horses back.

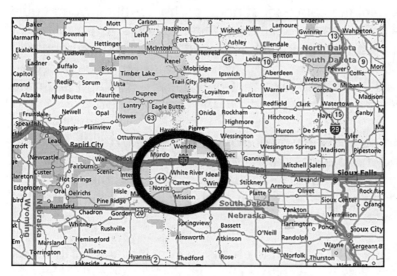

The next bronc rider to try them was Norm Mason, who was camped down on the river bottom just east of where Kenny Fox lives now. Norm had been a world-champion bronc rider in his days, but he was up in his 40's and these broncs just bucked too long and too hard for him to ride. Slim Jim crippled himself and was sold. Baxter Berry brought Pin Ears to the ranch.

At the White River Frontier Days Rodeo that fall, a cowboy by the name of Charlie Fallis won the bronc riding average. Bax hired him and brought him to the ranch; the first horse he put him on was Pin Ears. Pin Ears bucked him off, and quit buckin' about the time Charlie hit the ground. Charlie stayed around all fall and got to ridin' Pin Ears pretty regular. Pin Ears finally quit buckin'. Charlie quit there that winter, and the horse was put in Gib Peck's string. Gib rode him a long time, and seemed to get along real good. ●

THE YELLOW CAT HORSES

In the early 1900's, the government brought some horses from Idaho and Oregon to the Rosebud and Pine Ridge Indian Reservations in South Dakota. In that bunch of horses were a few yellow-hided horses. They had yellowish colored eyes and a yellow skin with little specks on it, kind of like an Appaloosa. Berry got a hold of a few of these mares, bred them to different kinds of studs, but down through the generations the horses that showed the yellow eyes and yellow hide seemed to be the best. About 1941, Paul Berry had a yellow-eyed gelding he called Kitten. At that time, White River, South Dakota had a pretty big rodeo they called Frontier Days. The Berry boys always went to the rodeo and took a string of horses. Paul took his yellow gelding with him, using him in several timed events. I think they won some calf ropin' and team ropin' money on him. There were some cowboys there from Oklahoma that had a good sorrel gelding they called Steeldust. They came and approached Paul about a matched race; they wanted to bet $50. Fifty dollars in 1941 was quite a lot of money, so Paul talked it over with Baxter, his brother, and Burl Phipps, his brother-in-law, and they decided that they'd match race him. At that time, White River had a race track, so they went down in front of the grandstand and stepped off 400 yards. The rules were that you walk your horses up to a big line in the sand side by side, then when you reached that line, you let your horse run. After several false starts, they finally got started. The Steeldust horse got the jump on Kitten, but when they crossed the finish line, Kitten out ran him by two lengths.

BILLY THE KID

"In 1967, I (Jim Abourezk) was appointed by the South Dakota Circuit Court to represent a client whom I will call Billy the Kid. Billy rustled cattle for a living, operating out of Shannon County. Although Billy lived on the Pine Ridge Indian Reservation, he was not an Indian. His specialty was loading the cattle he stole into a house trailer that he had adapted by cutting open the sides and top of the trailer's back wall to form a loading ramp. . ."

"He was finally caught on a day when he got a flat tire, prompting a friendly highway patrolman to stop to offer help. Naturally, the officer became suspicious at the sound of cattle mooing inside the lace-curtained house trailer and he arrested Billy, who began what was to be a long journey through the criminal justice system."

(Billy spent time on this and other charges in the South Dakota Penitentiary and later in Sandstone Federal Prison in Minnesota.)

"Although Billy had very little education, he was highly intelligent-street smart I believe is the proper description. He wrote on prison stationery a writ of *habeas corpus*, demanding his release . . .

"The federal judge, a Norwegian immigrant named Axle Beck, phoned me to ask if I would represent Billy. By then I had announced my candidacy for the Second District congressional seat . . .

"I prepared both a brief and my argument . . . Billy was brought down from Sandstone for the argument, looking pale from the long months spent in prison. When both the U.S. attorney and I was finished making our opposing cases, Judge Beck announced that he would need to review more case authority before he could decide the matter. . .

"My policy has always been that when I represented criminal defendants, I saw it as my responsibility to get them released from prison on bail. . .

"Your Honor,' I said in my most rational, and hopefully convincing voice, 'Billy has been wrongful imprisoned for more than two years now, and I think that he's entitled to be out on bail until your decision comes down.'

"I'll grant that request," Judge Beck Said. Everyone was shocked, including me. The U.S. attorney was, immediately on his feet, shouting his objections to the judge. The U.S. marshal who had brought Billy from Sandstone Prison shook a sheaf of papers in the judge's face.

"Judge – you can't turn him loose,' the marshall screamed, turning blue with rage. 'Nebraska wants him, everybody wants him. I've got the hold from Nebraska right here.'

"The marshall forgot the unbridle of power of federal judges. 'I don't care vot Nebraska vants,' Beck said, crashing his fist down onto the desk, 'he's gonna stay loose until I'm done vit him.'

"I hurriedly signed the bond form for Billy, hustled him to the Aberdeen airport, and bought him a ticket back to Rapid City before the prosecutor could think of a reason to have him arrested again. We landed at the Rapid City airport just after noon, and as we got into my car, I told Billy that I wanted to stop at a restaurant where the Democratic Forum was having a lunch meeting . . .

"Our now candidate for governor, Dick Kneip, is speaking today, and I'd like to try to hear at least the last part of his talk, Is it okay with you?" I asked.

"Billy couldn't say 'yes' fast enough. I had the feeling that he was so happy about being out of prison that he probably would have rubbed out someone had I asked him to.

"We were too late for the speech, and as we walked into the crowded dining room, Gene Bushnell, the president of the Forum announced that 'our candidate for Congress has just arrived.' Prompting applause from the partisan audience.

"As Billy and I found empty seats, I could hear Bushnell over the public address system saying, 'Jim, I see you have a guest with you today. Would you like to introduce him?"

"I winced. Although Billy had been out of the news for a couple years, his name had become a household word because of the publicity surrounding his burglary trail and his other escapes. He was so colorful that the newspaper and television newsmen had practically made a living running Billy the Kid stories.

"Yes,' I said, suppressing an impulse to run out of the room. 'I'd like to introduce Billy the Kid, my client, who just returned from Aberdeen with me.'

"As the Applause started, Billy stood up, obviously feeling a bit awkward and appearing unsure of himself. As it continued, however, he clasped his hands together in the same way that victorious prize fighters do, and held them above his head, acknowledging the audience's welcome.

"... the hapless Dick Kneip (who was elected governor that November) had no idea who he was. He came over to us after the meeting adjourned, greeting me and shaking my hand. He was equally effusive when he turned to Billy.

"Where are you from?" Kneip asked. "From Shannon County, sir,' Billy responded. "What kind of work do you do?' Kneip pressed on unsuspecting. "Uh . . . I'm in the cattle business, sir' Billy was uncomfortable.

"And where are you from, did you say?' Kneip was relentless.

"Well, actually, sir, I just got out of federal prison in Sandstone, Minnesota." Bill said.

"Kneip gulped, turned and literally ran to his car, unable to deal with what he surely saw as a negative association, something that might destroy his candidacy . . ."

Story written by Jim Abourezk ●

Printed with permission by Jim Abourezk.

LABOR DAY RODEO

Casey and I were going to a lot of SDRA rodeos; in the fall of 1974, we went to four during that weekend. The Labor Day rodeo was in Eagle Butte in the old tribal arena. It was cold, with the wind blowin' about 90 miles an hour straight across the arena out of the north. It was even blowin' little clods of dirt and rocks off the ground. It sure wasn't a fun rodeo, but about all the contestants were out tryin' to place for the year-end awards. Johnny Holloway and John Miller were pickin' up, and were havin' a tough time because of the wind. There were lots and lots of no-times in the roping events. It was hard to throw a rope against the wind, and there was a few times, but not very many; I can't remember how we done, but I don't think any good. I think there's one thing everybody remembered: Eddie Widow, an old Indian, and possibly his kid about 16 or 17, rode in the roping box. The kid had a little hat sittin' on top of a lot of black hair (and I don't know how he kept it there); he was ridin' an old one-eyed yellow horse.

The horse cranked his head around so's he could get his good eye on the steer, and you could tell he'd been roped off quite a lot before.

The horse cranked his head around so's he could get his good eye on the steer, and you could tell he'd been roped off quite a lot before. But lookin' at the kid brought smiles to everyone's face.

Page 112

But lookin' at the kid brought smiles to everyone's face. The kid nodded for his steer, and roped him around both horns just across the score line. Eddie rode in and double hocked him, and they went 10-9, and tied down team ropin'. Now generally to go 12 and below, everything has to be just right. They sure win the rodeo and wiped the smile off everybody's face.

Casey and I were played out, and were sure glad to see the ranch when we drove in around midnight that night, as we'd gone to a lot of rodeos and done ranch work both. It was sure good to see the rodeo season about at an end. ●

GATHERIN' STRAYS

In the fall of 1945, after they pulled the roundup wagon in, there were still quite a few cattle scattered around on the lease that had been missed during the roundup; and also some Antler cattle on some of the neighbors'. Bill Greenough had taken over as cow boss from his brother Frank, and Frank had bought a place down north of Gillette.

He sent me and Alvin Schaffer and a kid named Ted to go gather these cattle. We had an old Dodge Power Wagon for all our beds and equipment. The Antlers had built little traps (pastures) all over their lease to hold the night herd when the wagon was out, so we didn't have to stand guard. We would put the cattle we'd gathered in one of those little traps until we'd gathered 50-75 head, then we would trail them down to the Bighorn River by St. Xavier. The Bighorn was always swimming: we'd cross the cattle, and put them in a trap on Rotten Grass Creek, then we'd head back to gather more cattle. The kid quit about this time. Alvin and I went on gathering cattle. We finally ended up over in a neighbor's outfit. The fellow that was working there was a man by the name of Gilbert Brock; he had a trailer house for camp, which was really nice to a couple of cowboys who had spent about four and half months sleeping on the ground.

While there, we gathered quite a few steers. One day I was out alone and found eight-10 steers running with a bunch of cows. Now they took quite a lot of persuasion, but I finally got the steers cut out and headed toward camp, the way I wanted them to go. They had quit bothering me, and were trailing along really good. My horse was all sweated up, as it was a hot fall day, so I unsaddled him to let his back cool. I sat down on my saddle and rolled a smoke. Between my boots was a nice little bunch of dry grass. I sat there with a match in my hand. I'd always heard the oldtimers say that dry grass was like gunpowder, so I though to myself, "OBS", and dropped the match in that little bunch of dry grass. It just blew up, burned my eyebrows and eyelashes off, and some of my hair, my horse jerked away from me, I grabbed my saddle blanket and went to fighting fire. The only reason I got it out, was that when it came up out of the draw, the grass got pretty scarce. I went down and caught my horse, went to saddle up, and it had charred the under side of my saddle and burned the strings off. I really hated to go back to camp, as I knew those cowboys would really rib me, and I found out one thing: those oldtimers knew what they were talking about!

Now Alvin liked to play poker, so Gilbert and he would get out the cards about every night. Gilbert could do about anything with the cards; he would deal out four hands of five-card draw poker, then he would tell us what was in each hand, and he never made a mistake, time after time, with different games of poker. Alvin liked to go to Billings Montana and play poker. Gilbert kept telling him "You'd better stay home, because they're not going to let you win." He said "My dad's a poker player in Billings—that's how he makes his living, and he taught me how to do this."

Alvin and I stayed there about a week, and then we trailed the steers down to the river and swam them across. Alvin took the Power Wagon, went to the ranch, and quit. He headed for Billings to play poker.

I was on my own from then on. I packed my bedroll all over the Crow Indian Reservation on the back of a horse. My bed got to smelling like an old saddle blanket. When I went to the river to swim cattle across, as it got colder I had to break the ice on the edge where we went in, and on the opposite side where we came out. Ice wasn't very thick, but it had to be done. No matter how I tried to roll my bed up on the back of the horse, it still got wet. I would stay overnight in a little shack on Rotten Grass Creek. It generally took a little while to get to sleep in that cold, stinking, wet bed, but I was young and tough, and got along good.

I heard years later that Alvin got to be a stock detective and got in a gunfight around Hardin Montana, and was killed. Gilbert Brock later moved down around Martin, South Dakota and got to be a really good calf roper. He won a lot of money in the little amateur rodeos around the country. ♠

THE JOURNEY

After the Custer battle on the Little Big Horn, the hostile Indians scattered to the four winds. A big bunch went to Canada. With that group were two young Indian boys 16 or so years old. Their family lived on the Rosebud Indian Reservation on Black Pipe Creek. They were getting mighty homesick and wanting to go home. They knew the Cavalry was patrolling Montana. They had Crow and Ree scouts with them. They could read sign pretty well.

The boys decided to go anyway. They would go on foot without any

guns or horses. They thought if they did get caught the Cavalry would just think they were stragglers and let them go. All they took with them was a little jerky, an extra pair of moccasins and a knife. They traveled mostly by night, staying away from all the trails and very careful to leave no tracks at creek or river crossings.

They sat on her and ate raw liver and some raw meat. They finally started to get their strength back.

They traveled for about three weeks, running out of food and moccasins. One day they spotted an old buffalo laying in the head of a little draw. They went to look things over, being hungry and out of food. They were about ready to try anything. They snuck up on the buffalo and saw it was an old cow. The grass was tall around where the cow was laying. They got the wind right and snuck up on the old cow. When she started to get up, the one with a knife jumped on her back. The other one grabbed her by the tail. She went to bucking and kicking. But they stayed right with her. The one with the knife was stabbing the cow and they finally got her down.

They sat on her and ate raw liver and some raw meat. They finally started to get their strength back. They cut some meat and made some jerky by laying it on the grass around them to dry. They made some soles for their moccasins. They laid around for a couple of days getting rested up. Then they gathered up their jerky and started for home, being very careful and keeping out of sight. As they got closer to the reservation the Cavalry patrols got thicker and looking for anybody that was off the reservation. They finally made it back to Black Pipe Creek and to their families.

This story was told to me by Stanley Wooden Knife. The boy with the knife was his great grandfather.

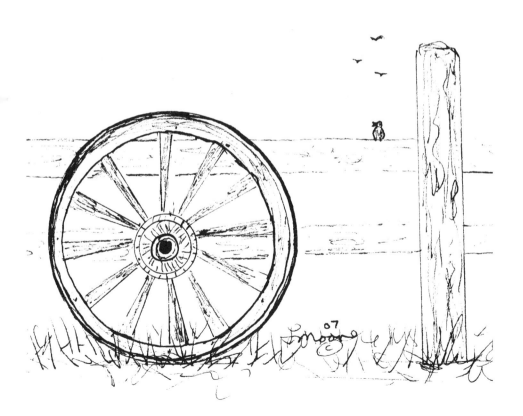

YELLOW DOG

I first ran into Yellow Dog the spring of 1949. We were working a bunch of colts; Paul Berry and I were teamed up in the round corral. We were four-footing colts, throwin' them down, brandin' and cuttin' them. The gate opened, and this little, short-aged yearlin' colt come into the corral. When he saw he was trapped, he laid his ears back and took a run at us. We chased him away, and when he ran around the corral, we four-footed him.

The colt belonged to Tom Berry, so we put a XX on the left shoulder. That evening, I asked Tom what he'd take for him. He said, "Give me $25 and he's yours." I wanted him because he had yellow-colored eyes, and his hide was yellow with little specks on it. I figured he was a throwback to the old yellow cat horses. I had hopes he'd turn out to be as good as most of them were. I broke him to ride the fall he was three, and rode him all winter. It was a hard winter, and I fed lots of hay with a team. I'd saddle up Yellow Dog and tie him to the back of the hayrack, and lead him around in case I would need him.

I quit that job in the spring, and made a deal to run on a place down by Presho South Dakota. The place was on the southwest corner of the Lower Brule Indian Reservation. I had about 70 cows and 250 yearlings on shares. I started ropin' some calves on him down there, and he got to workin' pretty good, so I went to a few rodeos. I always made a little money, as I mugged a lot of cows in the wild cow milking. I didn't rope so good, so muggin' cows really helped.

My next move was to the Pine Ridge Reservation. At one time, I had cows scattered from Wanblee to Bear Creek. I rode Yellow Dog pretty hard gatherin' up these cows. I finally got them gathered up in a bunch and branded the calves.

The next fall I moved my cows to Wounded Knee Creek. I made a deal with a fellow to run them for so much a month. I went to work on construction, as they were buildin' Interstate 90. I went up and looked at my cows around the first of March, and it looked like most of them were with calf but two or three. About the first of May, it got to rainin', and they stopped the roadwork, so I loaded up Yellow Dog and headed for Wounded Knee Creek. There were only 16 calves; somebody got off with the rest of them. It was quite a financial blow, as I had to sell down to pay the bank. About that time, Baxter Berry contacted me, and wanted me to work for him, so I moved my cows and everything to the XX Ranch. Bax had a high school boy working for him, and they needed a calf-roping horse, so I sold Yellow Dog to Bax. I last seen him the winter of 1978. The snow got deep, and the winter was tough; when spring came, I never could find him. ♠

OLD STYLE ROUNDUP

The range cattle business of the western United States was built around the chuck wagon. It came north with the great trail herds and stayed to become the hub of the large roundups that evolved as the cattle spread out to fill the vast ranges so recently occupied by the buffalo.

It has various names such as chuck wagon, grub wagon, or mess wagon and along with the bed wagon was about the only home the early day cowboy knew. With this and a great cavvy of horses, he worked the unfenced ranges.

The bed wagon carried the roundup beds, war bags, and usually a tent for bad weather. The canvas war bags held the few extra clothes, razor, and private things a cowboy might have.

To most modern cowboys "the wagon" is only a thing that dad or grandpa talked about and most large ranches are divided into enough pastures that no great roundup is required to gather any one pasture.

Even the remaining public lands have enough fences that large roundups are not needed in most places.

When pastures far from headquarters are worked, men and horses are moved by truck and trailer. Also, today's portable corrals or range-built corrals and traps greatly reduce the number of men and horses needed.

Even the good smell of burning wood is gone, since propane burners heat the branding irons and cook the grub. Also, few of today's cowboys have slept in a roundup bed, caught their mounts from a rope corral, or ridden a long circle.

One area where old methods are still used is deep in the red Stone Basin of the South Dakota Badlands where the Double X Ranch, belonging to Baxter Berry, and the Livermont spread, owned by Jerry and his dad, Sylvester, sprawl across parts of Mellette and Washabaugh counties on the Rosebud and Pine Ridge Indian reservations. The ranches cover more than the Red Stone Basin, but it is there the roundup camps are needed because of rough terrain and the isolation.

Late in October 1974, I came into Red Stone with the Berry wagon. Ahead, Berry's foreman, Ray Hunter, drove four good horses on the chuck wagon with a two-wheel stove trailer behind, and is a veteran of many roundups. It has escaped the rotting-down fate of most wooden wagons because of good care and a wagon shed at headquarters. With Ray was the roundup cook, Jim Ogle, Casey Hunter, Ray's son, and I were on the spring seat of the bed wagon pulled by a powerful team of blue roans. Behind us, Joe Stoddard, Paul Briggs, Lee Addison, Lonnie Carlson and Al Badure drove the extra saddle horses.

In the roughest country and at dry creek crossings, Joe rode ahead of the wagons to find the best ground. On steep descents, such as the pass into Red Stone Basin, log chains were used and help brake the heavy loads. In the miles between the Berry headquarters and the Red Stone campsite, the changes in terrain are abrupt: deep, timber-bottomed dry creeks; rough, grass covered hills; huge grass flats untouched by any plow; barren castle-like badland buttes; cedar-covered buttes; and distant pine ridges. Many-colored, strata-marked

badland walls rise from the floor of Red Stone and form its sides. They stop at the rim above, where the barren walls join the rich grass tables and benches.

As the wagons rolled, the jet age seemed to fade away. Even though I knew it would be brief, it was great to re-enter a time in history that I had lived as a youth.

The sun was low when we made our rendezvous with the Livermont wagon, cavvy, and cowboys. With the wagon were Jerry, Charlie Carlson, Joe and Sage Young, Roger Nieffer, Jerry Sharp and two bright-eyed boys who rode the wagon with their dads. They were Kevin Carlson and Wade Livermont. They proved to be popular boys in camp. Another who rode in that evening from his own ranch was Paul Brunch, a salty veteran cowboy of 64. Everyone pitched in to set up camp.

Soon the cook tent was pitched, extending back from the grub box at the rear end of the wagon. The stove was unloaded from the trailer that was unhooked and moved aside. Then the bid canvas fly was stretched over the entire wagon and extended several feet on each side. The cook tent and fly are luxuries many chuck wagons never has and make a very good camp, protected from the elements. With a big hot supper over, beds were rolled out and the camp settled down for the night.

The cook's alarm clock rang at 4:30 in the morning. Soon a hot wood fire had coffee made, biscuits baked, and bacon and eggs fried.

A rope corral tied to the bed wagon had been set up the night before and as soon as it was light enough to see, 40 horses were brought into the corral. In the half light, ropers started catching horses and soon everyone was mounted. Each rode a stout horse suitable for a long hard ride, and Ray Hunter carefully selected riders to go in pairs. Each pair was to cover certain areas in a way that the entire basin would be gathered.

Ray also instructed the cook that the men would be in late for dinner and some night be as late as two o'clock. Jim put together a huge stew that he could keep hot to fill the hungry punchers when they came in.

Lunch Break

With the cattle brought in from a long circle were six Double X steers that had spent the summer with a neighbor's cowherd. Hunter knew they would be hard to hold, so we ripped open burlap bags to use for hobbles. Cowboys soon caught the steers by the head and heels and stretched them out. Before long they were released with hobbles on their hind legs, which as Jerry said "should change their mind about sneaking off in the night."

Cowboy banter before bed that night was lively and often mixed with serious stories of things that happened on the long circles. It was easy to see that, hard as the work was, these young men were enjoying every minute, and in spite of what the jet age may do to the chuck wagon they would always have the best memories.

The cool gray dawn of the second day found everyone at the rope corral catching their best mounts to work the herd that had been brought in the day before. First the cows and calves were mothered up and sorted for brands. Jerry Livermont's were held in one bunch and his dad's in another. This work lasted until about noon, with riders on cutting horses carefully sorting the cattle while cowboys held the herds. Part of the crew rode into the wagon for dinner and fresh horses while the rest stood guard until their turn.

Charlie Carlson brought dry wood in from the creek in the bed wagon and soon a branding fire had hot irons ready. Ropers rode slowly through the herd to catch calves and drag them to the fire where calf wrestlers held them down to be branded. These had been born since the calf roundup in the spring. After the branding was done, the cows and calves were strung out in a long line to be counted, then turned loose to graze undisturbed until time to wean calves.

Next morning the work horses were caught from the rope corral and hitched to the already loaded wagons. I found myself alone on the bed wagon because Ray needed all hands mounted to drive home the Double X steers that had been gathered in the basin. It was great to drive a team of good horses and listen to something other than the roar of a motor.

Back at headquarters and after a late dinner in the big ranch house, I had a talk with Ray about what I believe to be one of the very last all-horse roundups.

How long would it be before a four-wheel drive pickup took the place of the faithful old chuck wagon? I wondered, how long before someone built a road into the basin so horses could be hauled in a truck or trailer? Is it practical to keep the old wagons going?

Ray did not hesitate with his answers. "We still have the wagons, work horses, and equipment in good shape. It makes a comfortable, practical camp. Because of terrain nothing modern can accomplish anything better, and besides, Baxter Berry wants to keep the wagon going so a few young men can have a true cowboy experience."

As for myself, I would hate to see the old wagons go. It is a last link with a truly great part of American history and besides, it has developed a group of young cowboys who have skills not learned with horse trailers, portable corrals, cattle chutes, calf tables, and arenas. ◖

Printed with permission of Western Horseman and Joy Neville, Copyrights August 1976

SHIPPIN' HOGS

When Berry's moved up on their homestead in Mellette County, South Dakota, they had 50-60 cows and a little bunch of mares. They done about everything to make a living. They bred the little mares to Percheron studs, as a broke team of horses would bring about $400 and they sold as many as they could.

I think about 1921 or so, Tom bought 80 or more sows. He just turned those sows out on the prairie like he did his cows, and they would pig out. The coyotes would try to get the little pigs, but the sows were pretty smart and pretty tough. He built a big hog pen at the ranch, and along in the fall, about the first of October, he'd start feedin' some corn in it. Those sows would bring their pigs in and stay close around so they could get at the corn. A few that didn't come in, a cowboy would ride out and start them in. Generally by the first of November all the hogs had come in. Berry's would work off the ones they wanted to keep, and turn the rest out; they'd get a double box wagon load of corn and throw a little corn around the wagon, and the pigs that were out would come and eat. Then they'd move the wagon a little ways and throw out a little corn, so every day they'd move the wagon a little further, throw out a little corn, then move it a little further. All those pigs would get to followin' it no matter where it went. It was about 15 miles in to the stockyards in Belvidiere. It would take about a week or so, but by feedin' a little corn and movin' the wagon, they would have all the pigs right in the stockyards, generally 500-600 pigs. I think they were shipped out of Belvidiere to a commission company in Sioux City, Iowa. Baxter told me at that time the hogs generally paid the leases and grocery bills, but they finally got to be such a nuisance that Berry's got rid of them. As time went on, if a cow laid down to have a calf, the sows would get to eating the calf as it was born. They'd slip around and suck a cow, and if you'd happen to leave your saddle or anything else out, they'd eat it too. There's nothing worse than a meat-eatin' hog.

THE TRIP

In the spring of 1934 my dad died. He was a World War I vet and was gassed while in France. He died a slow horrible death. As a little boy we would go and visit some of his old buddies in Hot Springs. The white sheets would be turned down with specks of blood all over them. My dad's lungs finally ruptured throwing blood all over him. We lived in Hot Springs so an ambulance was available. My mom sent for the ambulance and dad never came back. We had an old flat topped car and decided that we would go to California. The story at that time was my mother had an Aunt in California that had a farm. The Aunt thought my mother had some insurance money and my mother thought my Aunt with the farm was the place to go. But the Aunt was losing the farm and my mother had no insurance money.

There were three of us kids. I was six, my sister was 10, my brother was 13. There was another lady going that had two kids. To this day I don't know who they were. Us kids all got car sick. We would get sick just smelling a car because in those days the gas and oil smell was all over. The back window was out of the car and the dust would boil in through the back window. We got so we never stopped to throw up. We just passed a can and threw it out the window. Thirty miles an hour was top speed as the roads were just dirt. There were a lot of people on the road in old cars and pickups. Some had furniture tied on them. We were most all headed the same way. Everybody was mad, mean, and broke. In those days if you had a flat tire you had to fix it right along side the road. Now those two women and my brother didn't know how to fix a flat. We might set alongside the road for hours with all those cars going by and nobody would stop. If they did stop to fix the flat, they wanted something for doing it, generally money. That was something I believe we were short on.

As a little boy I was sick, tired, dirty, and I wanted to stop somewhere and swim. Water was a priority. The old car got hot and you would have to have water. Not everybody would let you have water. If you stopped to get gas, generally they would let you have water, but they rationed it. So you had a hard time getting enough water to drink and keep the old car going. So they kept telling me when we got to the Great Salt Lake that I could go swimming.

When we got there it was about four inches deep and full of salt brine. They tried to talk me out of going swimming, but I was determined to find water somewhere. I waded out in the lake for a long, long ways and finally just sat down and went to bawling. I finally got up and waded back out. But that day changed my life forever.

We finally got to the Aunt's farm in northern California. My mother left us kids there and went back to South Dakota. An old family friend Tom Berry gave my mother a job working in the State House.

Us kids stayed in California for approximately a year working around the farm mostly picking strawberries. Finally my mother sent for us to come home, but only to run into another catastrophe. My mother had met another man and had gotten married. He didn't want us kids around. So we were put out for room and board. That pretty much was the end of our family ties. ♠

THE DOUBLE X COWS

Baxter Berry was an old cowboy rancher. About everything was done on horseback or with a team. He knew the art of riding bad horses and staying healthy. One of his main interests was breeding good range cattle, cattle that had a lot of liveability, that were thrifty, and could take care of themselves. He experimented with a lot of different breeds. I don't believe Baxter ever pulled a calf or sewed up a prolapsed cow. I never saw him on a tractor, but he had a little tractor that an Indian boy named Jumbo mowed hay with. When Jumbo brought the tractor home in the fall, Baxter had him park it in a gravel pit so nobody would see it.

Baxter bought some Scotch Highland cattle, had some of them imported from Scotland, and also bought some purebred longhorn cattle which at that time were hard to find. He also imported some "cracker cows" from Florida and some Mexican cows out of Mexico. He had a few Brahmas, and even had an Afghander which were a cherry red cattle with a corkscrew horn. He crossed these cattle all different ways, and some of them were awful bronky. The Scotch Highland cattle were the most protective of their baby calves. Bax crossed them on longhorns, with a little Brahma mixed in. You didn't brand these calves without cutting the cows away first.

Baxter Berry and Jerry Livermont had a lease together over in Redstone Basin. When I ran the ranch in the 1970's, we always went over with a roundup outfit to work those cattle. Baxter had sold Jerry a bunch of these cows. One fall Jerry had about thirty late calves that he wanted to brand. With no corral around, we had to figure out how we were going to do it. We took the bed wagon out and parked it not too far from the herd of cattle, took the team off about a hundred yards and hobbled them. Over by the team, we built a branding fire. A cowboy would ride in, rope a calf around the neck, and drag it to the bed wagon, throw the slack of the rope up over the bed wagon where two calf wrestlers in the bed wagon could get a hold of him. All the time, the cow would be bawling, chasing around the bed wagon, and hooking it (as most of these cows were horned). We had a cowboy sitting over by the branding fire on horseback. When they got the calf down in the bed wagon, the man at the fire would hand him a hot iron, and he'd lope over to the bed wagon and give the iron to the brander who was in the wagon. Sometimes the roper would have to ride back in and coax the cow into chasing him so the rider with the branding iron could get near the wagon.

A few years later, I was ranching in the southern Hills and had a bunch of this same kind of cows, only some of these had some Hereford in them. My neighbor, Gene Phillips, wanted to trap some coyotes in the pasture where these cows were running. In a month or so, I saw Gene and asked him how his trapping was coming: he said "I pulled my traps, as every time I caught a coyote, when I checked my traps, there'd be nothing but a few scraps of hide around. Your cows would come and tromp the coyote to death." This same bunch of cows summered on a high plateau down by the Cheyenne River. There was no water on the plateau, so they'd have to go down to the river for water. Down off that plateau to the river was a trail about three-quarters of a mile long that was pretty much straight up and down. They got so they wouldn't come to water but every three days, and the calves that fall averaged 500 pounds.

MY FAMILY

The stories in this book are mostly stories I heard from old-timers and things that have happened to me over a period of years cowboying and working on ranches, and ranching on my own, so maybe I'd better add a little about my family.

The Hunters came to the Black Hills of South Dakota in the 1890's and settled around Custer. They were frontiersmen, trappers, and they also did a little mining. The Black Hills at that time didn't look like they do now. The valleys were all stirrup-deep with grass, and not nearly the timber there is now. My dad was born in Newcastle, Wyoming in 1893. He left home as a young man and went to stay with some people named Callan. Two of the Callan boys were near my dad's age, named Stan and Harry. At that time, in that area of Wyoming, there were lots of big ranches, and these boys went to work cowboying for those ranches. They worked mostly on horse outfits, which paid five dollars more a month. They bunched horses up on the flat, like you did cattle in those days, and roped the colts and unbranded horses around the neck, dragging them to the branding fire. With two men to a team, one on the head would reach over the rope, grab the colt by the nose, and fall over backwards; the other man would grab a back leg and hold him down just like you would a calf. Someone would come and brand and castrate the colt, then they'd turn him loose.

The Black Hills at that time didn't look like they do now. The valleys were all stirrup-deep with grass, and not nearly the timber there is now.

In the summer if they were home, Dad, Stan and Harry went to all the ballgames around the area. If anybody thought they had a bucking horse, they'd generally bring him along too. After the ballgame, they would pass a hat to get enough money to pay a rider; then they'd lead the horse out onto the ball field, snub and blindfold him, and saddle him up. That's how they picked up a little extra cash in the summer time. If they had a really tough horse, they generally got Harry to ride him, because he was considered the best rider.

A few years later, Stan, Harry, and my dad each settled on what was called a "wilderness homestead," which was 640 acres, and these joined each other. When the war came along in 1917, my dad enlisted in the army, and was gassed during combat in France.   He met and married my mother in 1919; she was a Hollenbeck from Pringle. They were married November 9, and it snowed all that day. They rode out to his homestead, and the next morning it was still snowing, and the snow was up to the bottom of the windows.

My mother's dad was a depot agent who came to Deadwood in 1905, a year before the railroad got there, to help establish a depot; and later was depot agent in Mystic, Rochford, then Pringle. The depot in Pringle had a big second floor. My grandmother and other women around Pringle arranged dances about once a month. They would cook up all kinds of grub, with big tubs full of fried chicken. Everybody would dance all night, then eat supper, get in their buggies and on their horses, and head for home. The oldtimers told me my mother and her older sister were the belles of the Southern Hills. A cowboy, miner, or lumberjack would ride 50 miles just to dance with them; so Mother had lots of suitors, some of them welcome and some of them not! One was an outlaw gunman everybody in the area was scared of. The sheriff had a warrant for his arrest, but was scared of him. When the outlaw went to the outhouse behind one of the bars in Pringle, the sheriff and the deputy slipped up, one on each side of the outhouse, and shot him while he was inside.

**Hunter, in his younger years, lived with many
different families. His father had died when
Ray was young and Ray's mother left him with
various "foster parents."**

In the spring of 1920, my dad and mother sold the ranch at Pringle for ten dollars an acre, and bought a place down on the Rosebud Indian Reservation in Mellette County, South Dakota not far from the little town called Cedar Butte. Dad trailed his cows in there from Custer County and began ranching in that area. His first neighbors were Cleve and Tom Berry. They worked cattle together and became friends, and I think the friendship lasted for two generations. My dad's getting gassed in the war made him sick, and he just kept getting sicker, until he finally sold the ranch, and bought a meat market in a little town called Norris. He finally got too sick to even run the meat market, so they moved to Hot Springs in 1932 when Tom Berry was governor.

Tom gave all his old cowboy friends jobs, including my dad, who was assistant director of Custer State Park until he died in 1934.

MY LITTLE RANCH

When I turned 74, I leased a little ranch up on the North Moreau River north of Mud Butte, South Dakota. It was a beautiful ranch with quite a lot of grass, with that little river running the full length of it. I could run a hundred cows on it, and it was so easy to operate I had lots of time. About every morning in the spring and summer, I'd go out on the porch with a cup of coffee, and listen to the sounds of nature. There were quite a lot of deer and antelope in the country, which I could watch from my front porch. Wild turkeys came up round about two or three times every spring, but they didn't stay long, as there wasn't enough timber for them. My saddle horses were in a little pasture right in front of the house, and all I had to do in the morning was holler at them, and I had a grulla horse that would come on a lope, and bring the rest of the horses with him. About the only work I had to do was to put in a river crossing once in a while, and look after a little fence. In the winter time, I caked my cows as they ran on grass all the time; along that little river, after they got located, I never had to open water. I had a little calving pasture right by the barn; it was easy to look after them while they were calving. I fed a little bit of hay to them at that time. I had that little ranch leased for two years. My body was getting worn out, and I knew if we got into a bad winter, I wouldn't be able to take care of my stock, so I decided to sell out. I loved that little ranch; it was a great place.